God's provisions for the holy life
EVERYTHING NECESSARY

LUKE KEEFER, JR. *Roxbury Camp*
Aug. 4, 1987

Dear Harold & Catherine,
Thanks so much for your friendship through the years. God bless you both, your family, and your continuing ministries.

Luke L. Keefer, Jr.

Published by

Evangel
Press

301 N. Elm St.
Nappanee, Indiana 46550

A leader's guide, prepared by John R. Yeatts (Assistant Professor of Christian Education at Messiah College, Grantham, Pa.) is available to assist in group study of this book.

Copyright © 1984 by Evangel Press
Printed in the United States of America

ISBN: 0-916035-12-3

Contents

Foreword

I have often wished that Sunday morning sermons needed no title for the worship bulletin. That feeling persists now in regard to this book. The expression "the holy life" seems so open to misunderstanding. It evokes images of Eastern religions, Christian monasticism, or "holier-than-thou" postures which offend many Christians. Why should one even bother to write on such a subject? Or, to put it differently, if the subject itself is timely, why encumber it with such a perilous title?

It would seem, on the surface, to be sufficient to talk about "the Christian life," for that is the real substance of the topic under discussion. But, upon reflection, that will not prove adequate for several reasons. First, the word "Christian" is much too plastic. It gets pressed into such widely different molds that its usefulness becomes questionable. Nearly everything or almost nothing can be covered by the same term. We need something more precise if discipleship today is going to be addressed in light of the New Testament mandates of the kingdom.

Secondly, the Bible describes and illustrates what the life of the people of God *ought* to be. It lifts up the mature Christian model as something to which all Christians should aspire. It insists upon a standard that calls into judgment digressions from the will of God for his people. In order that we do not decide upon the meaning of the Christian life through some sort of Christian opinion poll (or average Christian life index), it seems helpful to use some term that causes us to feel the impact of the "upward call of God in Christ Jesus" (Philippians 3:14 RSV). The expression "the holy life" is intended to serve that purpose in this book.

Thirdly, we recognize that our understanding of the Christian life has been shaped by the heritage which has brought us to faith. For those of us influenced by Anabaptist, Pietist, and/or Wesleyan roots, "the holy life" appropriately captures much of our understanding of the nature of the Christian experience and style of life. It is for us a summary codename for both the thrust of New Testament discipleship and the spiritual heritage which has nourished us.

Briefly stated, the holy life is a *vision*—a compelling vision of the model for living that Jesus left his disciples. It is a *desire*—an aspiration to pursue that vision and be controlled by it. It is a *discipline*—a conscious effort to take the steps necessary to accomplish the goals of discipleship. It is a *discovery*—the realization that God cares more about the quality of our Christian life than we do. Moreover, God has done far more through Christ to guarantee our success than we can fathom.

Everything Necessary: God's Provisions for the Holy Life is a statement describing God's grace. It is not a description of this book, for the study here is introductory at best. The title affirms a view of God as the loving Father who does not lay greater burdens on his children than they can bear. A truly magical moment for some Christians occurs when they discover that God's resources for spiritual life are adequate for all the demands of discipleship he has laid upon us. For only when God is Lord of resources as well as Lord of requirements is he really Lord of all. The holy life begins, continues, and culminates in Christ. It is the miraculous power of his grace that transforms us into his kind of people.

Chapters one through three attempt to develop several concepts which help us define the holy life. Chapters four through ten discuss the conditions (methods, steps) of the holy life, helping us understand how spiritual formation and transformation occur. The final two chapters look to the goal of the holy life, trying to suggest the ultimate purposes of the holy life. Thus, in sequence, the questions of What? How? and Why? are raised in regard to the holy life.

The book is written primarily for those who will read it in the course of small-group studies (i.e., Sunday school classes, Bible study groups, etc.). Therefore, it has no pretentions of being an exhaustive statement. Neither is it intended to sell a particular theological system or program of Christian experience. Rather, the intention of this study is to enable Christians to wrestle with basic issues, discussing the implications of these issues for their own lives. It assumes readers really want their Christian life to be vital and growing. For as Samson was able to find honey in a lion's carcass (Judges 14:8-9), such readers will find something helpful in spite of the limitations of the study. If serious Christians find a measure of benefit in the book, the author's efforts will have been rewarded.

Luke Keefer, Jr.

Acknowledgments

No one can write reflectively without being conscious of the profound debt he owes to numerous people. The problem is that many cannot be thanked by name. Space limitations alone rule out many names worthy of credit. On a deeper level, what we are and how we think and talk is largely the result of countless influences upon our lives. Here one can be forgetful or simply not conscious of those whose influence has been the greatest resource for a particular idea or conviction. Until the rewards of heaven mete out full justice, I must be content to express thanks anonymously to a host of people who are part of this book.

I do wish to consciously pay tribute to several groups of people who have invested heavily in this project. The editorial committee, composed of J. Wilbur Heisey, Simon Lehman, Jr., Glen Pierce, and John Yeatts, has invested many days in reading various copies of the manuscript, discussing them with me, and giving valuable suggestions for improvements. Extensive kindness has pervaded their criticisms.

A volunteer Sunday school class from my local congregation, the Harrisburg Brethren in Christ Church, has gone through the chapters with me in a quarter of study. This "laboratory experiment" for the book has provided helpful feedback for the revision process of the various chapters. I express gratitude to and appreciation for Rhoda Carr, Rodney Chamberlain, Cara Musser, Lyle Myers,

Brengle Waldron, and Dallas and Diane Wolgemuth. They have been a strong source of affirmation for me in this task.

Messiah College has also contributed to this project in many respects. I have been granted time to write, furnished with a study carrel in the library, and granted funds to cover the costs of preparing initial drafts of the book. I am grateful to the staff of the faculty services office, Mrs. Bonnie Ganoe, Mrs. Judy Armacost, and Miss Karen Brasted, for the investment of their expertise as they translated my "hieroglyphics" into English print. Mrs. Armacost, in particular, labored through the entire first draft during the hot summer of 1983. And in the frigid January of 1984, under the pressures of my publication deadlines and her full-time class load, she pushed through the necessary revisions of most of the chapters.

The management and staff of Evangel Press have expended countless hours in getting the manuscript into book form. I deeply appreciate their labor and the fine spirit of cooperation they have exhibited on this project.

Greatest thanks must go to my wife, Doris, and our sons Brian and Dale. All the others mentioned previously have borne with the book in some fashion or other. My family has had to bear with the author. They alone have had to endure the schedule and the nerves of one who writes. Since they have been called to the greatest sacrifice, they merit my deepest thanks.

Luke Keefer, Jr.

Like newborn babies, crave pure spiritual milk, so that by it you may grow up in your salvation . . .

But solid food is for the mature, who by constant use have trained themselves to distinguish good from evil.

1 Peter 2:2; Hebrews 5:14

1

A Good Beginning

1 Peter 1:22-2:3; Hebrews 5:11-6:3

It is Sunday, August 20, 1978. The hour is late, and yet I cannot sleep. The tranquil setting of Niagara Christian College on the bank of the Niagara River is not enough to lull me to rest. Neither is the early alarm setting for a tomorrow full of speaking appointments a sufficient threat to drive me to slumber. Every time I close my eyes, hoping that dreams will overcome a reluctant body, I relive the scenes of the day. The birth of one's first child is a fantastic experience! Such scenes are etched on granite; they endure the effacing effects of time.

Christian conversions are in a similar category. When believers have proclaimed the gospel of salvation—whether to their children in the church or to their unchurched friends—there is great anticipation of the time when faith shall come alive and bear fruit in a conscious decision to follow Christ. Every "new birth" in the spiritual realm is a cause for celebration. Jesus said the angels in heaven rejoice when one sinner repents (Luke 15:7); and the church on earth is scarcely less festive. Birth-days, physical and spiritual, are days to remember!

The celebration of birth

In the first elation of childbirth, one stands in awe of the life God has given. There is a natural impulse to give thanks and to announce the good news. Everything which is to follow depends upon this initial gift of life. In like fashion, spiritual development depends upon the miracle of the new birth. Once God has given life to the soul, our care for and nurture of this believer aids growth and development. But apart from the life of salvation, there is nothing to nurture. A stillborn child can never be made to live and grow, despite our best efforts. Conversion, then, is to be celebrated as the necessary beginning of the Christian life.

We could not imagine someone visiting in our home and criticizing our baby for not having the full stature nor the complete abilities of an adult. Children are to be judged by the measure of a child and not the standards of an adult. Persons new to the family of God, likewise, are to be received with joy into the Christian fellowship. While they are not mature in their faith—and will not be so for some time—they are legitimate members of the family. They deserve the attention and the celebration that pertains to "babes in Christ."

Growth is expected

Even before we recover from the excitement of birth, our thoughts turn toward the future. The child we cradle in our arms forces such thoughts upon us. These little creatures are packed full of potential. Their eyes are made for sight, and they have ears for hearing. Their mouths are fashioned for speech. They have hands to reach and to grasp, and in due course their feet will walk. And so we plan for and dream of what they will become. This beginning which we celebrate is but the first stage in a long-term process of life.

Growth and development is so much a part of natural life that we take it for granted. We seldom give it much thought unless there is some noticeable departure from the expected. A vastly accelerated growth or an abnormally retarded development would gain our attention simply because it does not appear to be "normal." Otherwise, we expect the stages of infancy, childhood, adolescence, adulthood, and old age to succeed one another in the regular course of life.

Similar expectations hold true for the Christian life as well. However, the growth stages are not as well defined as they are for the natural process; neither are we as scientifically precise about the amount of time and experience required to move from one stage to another. The Bible gives some indication of the characteristics of "babes in Christ" and also of those who are "mature in Christ." Most Christians seem to be somewhere in between these stages, judging from the general tenor of the scriptural instruction for believers.

This does raise certain cautions in regard to expectations for growth. Each of God's creatures seems to have a built-in timeclock. If we try to pressure them into faster development, we may do more harm than good. The youthful David could use the shepherd's slingshot to kill Goliath, but if he had gone into the battle weighted down with Saul's armor, one wonders what the outcome would have been. Sometimes children do not mature as fast as parents would like them to. But many parents have discovered that attempting to force growth is more likely to bring out additional immature behavior than it is to produce positive growth. If our concern is to see genuine spiritual development, then we must learn to respect God's sense of timing in each individual life.

Who is responsible for growth?

The fact that the Bible calls new believers "babes in Christ" underscores the fact that they have a great degree of dependency upon spiritual parents for their nurture. At the same time, there is the element of individual responsi-

bility of each Christian for the steps of obedient discipleship in his or her life. Both the group and the individual
share in this responsibility for spiritual growth. As a general rule, however, the spiritual growth here parallels that
of natural development. Thus, as persons mature in
Christ, they assume increasing responsibility for their
own spiritual formation.

The church's responsibility for growth

Jesus' great commission (Matthew 28:19-20) makes
the instruction of converts as much a part of the church's
task as that of evangelism. Only the most negligent of
parents would bring children into the world and then
assume no responsibility for their care. Nurture involves a
much more extensive commitment than evangelism.
Thus, the apostles of Christ kept in touch with their
converts through visits, letters, and the appointment of
leaders capable of caring for their spiritual children. In this
way, the earliest converts to Christianity received the
instruction, love, and modeling of the early church.

The Apostle Peter identifies the Word of God as the
"spiritual milk" that newborn babes are to desire (1 Peter
1:23-2:2). If we wish to see people grow toward spiritual
maturity, then it is the responsibility of the church family
to nourish converts in the Word of God. Whether this
happens in one-on-one Bible studies, in group studies for
new converts, or in the more traditional church structures
and meetings, it is an essential task of the church. Even
more, it is the duty of the church to teach young believers
how to study the Bible meaningfully on their own. Moni-
toring the spiritual diet of Christians is as serious a
responsibility as supervising the dietary needs of our
children. There is a direct correlation between believers'
instructional diet and their spiritual development.

Just as children need affection and affirmation for

healthy emotional growth, so do young converts, in order to relate well to their spiritual pilgrimage. Young Christians need a family of faith where people "love one another deeply, from the heart" (1 Peter 1:22). They need to experience such love to know that they belong to the group and are welcomed there. They need healing care when bruised by life and affirmation when doubting their status or abilities. They need to experience trust as they exercise gifts for ministry in keeping with their development. They must be restored in tenderness when they falter and fail. Individuals who experience a loving support group can absorb considerable adversity in life and yet aspire to great accomplishments. Love is essential to growth.

The church needs persons who can serve as models of Christian discipleship to those younger in the faith who are seeking a pattern for their spiritual growth. However, it can be a frightening experience to be a parent, especially when you realize that your children follow your example more than your teaching! (Or is it not rather that people learn better from examples than they do from words?) Nevertheless, Paul put his Christian life on the line and told his converts to follow him as he imitated Christ (1 Corinthians 4:16; 11:1; Philippians 3:17). He told Timothy to be a worthy example of the Christian life to those under his ministerial care (1 Timothy 4:11-16). Behind every story of spiritual success, one generally discovers the influence of exemplary individuals or caring groups who modeled true discipleship for young believers (1 Thessalonians 1:6; 2:14; Hebrews 6:12). Good models have a magnetic effect upon other believers.

Individual responsibility for growth

From the earliest stages of infancy, children reflect individual personalities. Thus, those raised in similar ways in the same family react differently to their training and grow at different rates. With maturation also comes an increasing individual responsibility to determine the direction in one's life and the pace for achieving it. The Bible recognizes human responsibility in Christian development and addresses its message to the choices we need to make.

Ordinarily the term "babes in Christ" has nothing unpleasant associated with it. All new Christians begin the Christian way as novices. When Paul called the Corinthian believers "spiritual babes," however, it was a different matter. They were failing to live as Spirit-filled believers. Instead they followed their carnal desires, acting in some respects like the non-Christians around them (1 Corinthians 3:1-4). Paul lamented the fact that they were not yet ready to eat solid food. He still had to feed them milk. One senses Paul's disgust with these infantile Christians. They had known the gospel long enough to be much further along in their development than they actually were.

The writer to the Hebrews shares a similar outlook (5:11-6:3). Here were believers who seemed content to rest at the starting-block of their Christian race. They did not want to hear how they could finish the race to maturity in their faith. In their careless indifference to the deeper truths of the Word, they were becoming like barren soil, in danger of being judged for their unfruitful lives. They were no longer following the example of faith that the more mature people of God had exhibited. Spiritual sluggishness had become the attitude of their life.

In both cases we see God's displeasure with Christians whose growth was far below his expectations. God holds these people responsible for their condition. It was not a matter that they had not reached all their spiritual aspirations as yet. Paul says that even the most mature Christians still sense a gap between their aspirations and their accomplishments (Philippians 3:12-16). The people addressed in Corinthians and Hebrews were not even aspiring to growth, nor were they exerting the effort necessary to follow Christ fully. They were content to be stunted in their moral development, to be mere babes when they should have been approaching adulthood. Spiritually, they were asleep. The stern voice of Scripture tried to awaken them to their personal responsibility to grow up in Christ.

Two kinds of growth statements

Spiritually as well as physically, there are two kinds of people: those who grow within the boundaries of expected development and those who do not. Both are in need of instruction concerning their growth, but the messages are vastly different in the two cases.

There are many passages of Scripture addressed to Christians who are walking acceptably with God. They challenge us to greater growth, usually by means of encouragement to our faith. No Christian ever gets to the point where he or she no longer needs these instructions.

The passages addressed to believers whose growth is delinquent have a different tone. They carry a note of serious concern. Unless there are decisive actions taken, these people's walk with God stands in jeopardy. In applying the Scripture, we must see to it that the proper message gets to the right persons.

Christian maturity and the holy life

The goal of the holy life is that all Christians would "in all things grow up into . . . Christ" (Ephesians 4:15). That is the purpose of this book. We will note the general principles of spiritual formation that apply to those who desire to follow the Lord. Where we are in our Christian development is not the crucial issue. If we are walking obediently to God's present expectations, we are already experiencing a vital dimension of the holy life.

On the other hand, we must reckon with the sad fact that many believers suffer from stunted growth. By the miracle of the new birth, they began their Christian life well. But for one reason or another, their spiritual life has stagnated. This book seeks to probe some of the causes of this retarded growth and some of the cures that God offers to remedy them. Perpetual spiritual babyhood is unacceptable to God. God wants all his children to come to maturity in their Christian life.

How great is the love the Father has lavished on us, that we should be called children of God! And that is what we are!

1 John 3:1

2

Learning Your Christian Names

Ephesians 1:1-10; 1 John 3:1-10

Naming children is sometimes viewed as a casual matter in Western society. We simply do not realize how much names affect people. Think what happens, for example, to children when they go to school. Some have names that are difficult to spell. Others have names which confuse sexual identity, or at least make it ambiguous. Some names sound funny and make classmates laugh, or invite corruptions which replace the real name in youthful conversation. Thus, some children are negatively conditioned by their names, and life for them is made more difficult.

On the other hand, certain names have greater social acceptance. Strange as it may seem, those who are fortunate enough to have such names tend to do a little better in school, find better jobs, and are generally more successful in all their endeavors in life. Naming children after people who are admired in a given family or culture can have the same effect. It gives them a name to live up to in their life. A good name actually helps to shape a good person!

In reading the Bible, one is struck by the importance attached to names. Parents gave careful thought about names for their children, and God often instructed them to give a child a particular name. Names were associated with character: a reflection of the kind of person one was or would be. Thus, if a person's character changed significantly, a new name—or at least a surname—was considered a necessity.

If we understand this significance in names, we are prepared to understand something of the dynamics of spiritual life. When one becomes a Christian—in scriptural terms, is born into or adopted into the family of God—he or she inherits a name (or names). As in natural life, so in spiritual life, one receives a family name and a given name. These names affect our life and character and, to a large extent, shape our understanding and experience of the holy life.

"Christian" is a family name

The family name one inherits has a long history to it. It represents an accumulation of experience that has established certain traditions. Sometimes it is associated with a particular location or a family trade. Certain family practices have become established, holiday observances being a case in point. Particular values, points of view, styles of life, and even speech patterns belong to the family and are passed on to each new arrival. Families pass on a social code as much as they do a genetic code. Thus in spite of differences due to individual personalities and particular life histories, there are discernable family traits shared in common by all its members.

The simple fact that a son arrives in family X rather than family Y will have enormous impact upon the kind of person he will be. Long before the child makes determinations for himself, his family will already have shaped the direction of his thought. If the family bond is strong and positive, it will continue to influence the choices the individual makes for himself. Consciously or unconsciously, a person often tries to fit the mirror image of his family.

Think then what it means to be a Christian. It is a codeword for a whole set of values by which one lives.

Centuries of biblical revelation and Christian history lie behind the word. Family traditions are established, and there are family traits discernably different from any other association. When one becomes a Christian, he is influenced as much by this family name—and all it stands for—as any birth into a human family. The Christian community is a family mold that will shape his life consciously and unconsciously. The individual, in turn, will seek to imitate the family image, in order to live up to the family name he has inherited.

The word "Christian" as used today combines the ideas of many New Testament terms for members of God's family. Christians were called believers because they believed that Jesus, the Son of God, was God's appointed Messiah to provide salvation—the only means whereby sinners could be brought into the family of God. Christians were also called disciples because they followed the example and teaching of Jesus, imitating his way of doing God's will in a world corrupted by sin. And these words still are applied to Christians as descriptive and formative terms.

There is another term, however, that deserves special study here because of its linguistic connection with the holy life. It is the noun "saint" (literally the "holy one"), from which comes also the verb "to sanctify" and the noun "sanctification." In both the Old and New Testament, God's people are referred to as "saints." Initially it meant those people—or even things—devoted (consecrated) to God's service. Since God was absolutely holy, there was a developing consciousness that those who served God should be holy as well. Thus, in the course of biblical usage, the word picked up the idea of purity as well as that of consecration.

A careful study of the way the Bible uses the word "saint" highlights two important aspects. First, the word

"saint" is a relational term. Only God is holy; mankind is
sinful. People are "holy" only because of their right relationship with God. This is another way of saying salvation
is by grace. Neither you nor I make ourselves holy and
thus win God's approval. We are brought into God's family through Jesus' saving act and thus declared to be holy,
belonging to God. In like manner, one obtains a family
name either by birth or adoption. You can only be a Smith,
for example, by actual relationship in the Smith family.

Secondly, the word "saint" is a group word, a true
family name. Since medieval times people have tended to
think of "saints" as a special class of Christians: unusual,
extraordinary believers. In the Bible it is a family name,
seldom used in the singular number, a word for the total
group of God's people. If we have the eyes for it, there is an
important clue here concerning the holy life. The holy life
is a group (family) activity; it is the collective task of the
church to live to God's honor and help each of its members
to so achieve that goal.

Now, the interesting thing about the family name
"saint" is that it connotes both what believers are *and* what
they ought to be. The Greek expression at both Romans
1:7 and 1 Corinthians 1:2 could be translated either "those
who are called (named) saints" or "those who are called to
be saints." This is a wonderful ambiguity, for the Bible
stresses both aspects of our family name.

Perhaps an illustration would be helpful at this point.
Each member of the Williams family received the family
name, and all the rights pertaining to it, when he or she
entered the family. But not every member exhibits fully all
the honorable traits that belong to the reputation of the
Williams family. At one and the same time each person is a
Williams and is becoming a Williams.

The Christian family name "saint" works in precisely
the same manner. Every child of God has been made holy

through the redemption provided in the blood of Christ. Past sins have been forgiven (Ephesians 1:7), and the believer has been cleansed (sanctified = made holy) from the corrupt practices of the former life in sin (1 Corinthians 6:11). So thorough is the transformation—from the former life of sin to that of a member of God's family— that Paul likens it to a death and resurrection (Romans 6:1-11). The result is that one does not go on sinning. John explains this mystery by a birth metaphor, saying that offspring resemble their parents, since they bear their parents' genetic code (i.e., "like father, like son"). Since the God who begat us does not sin, we who are God's children will not continue to practice sin in our lives (1 John 3:4-10).

Yet, each child of God longs to more fully realize the life of the "saints." In spite of the vast change that conversion brings, those young in the faith do not immediately achieve all the characteristics of the family name. Frequently there is the realization that not all of one's actions, much less yet one's attitudes, are saintlike (Christian). Moments of insight reveal areas of the personality that have not yet heard the gospel of Jesus Christ. Even where we feel good about our faith and service, there is yet the knowledge that it could be better.

The desire then to fill out one's Christian character, to grow up in Christ in every way (Ephesians 4:15), to strive with all the saints to make the church, the people of God, what it ought to be—this is the quest for the holy life. Paul expresses this attitude well in the first chapter of Ephesians, where he talks about God's purpose in choosing us to be his children. It is that we might be "holy and blameless in his sight" (verse 4), that we should live "to the praise of his glorious grace" (verse 6), fitting in with God's plan to finally unite all things to himself, both in heaven and on earth (verse 10). Those who are Christ's have felt this drawing of the Holy Spirit toward the full realization of the meaning of our family name "Christian." With rejoicing that God has called us his own, we press on to obtain the Christlike life, so that Christ might not be ashamed to own us as his brethren.

Our individual "given name"

Children receive not only the family name but also a given name that distinguishes them from other members of the family. This is in recognition of the individual worth and unique contributions of every person in the human family. It allows individuals the room to develop an identity within the context of the larger family.

Here, too, there are important implications for an understanding of the holy life. The same spiritual pilgrimage is not experienced by all Christians in the same way. Any family that has spent a vacation in travel understands this. One family member is enthralled with scenic beauty, another is engrossed in historical sites, while a third is constantly making friends of new people encountered in the travel. Since the itinerary is a shared experience, the members of the family can discuss the trip with common feelings and experiences. But in another sense, each experienced a trip that none of the others shared. Likewise the holy life is a group experience with multiplied features which are shared endeavors. Yet it can never be stereotyped into a rigid format of sterile sameness. Each of us pursues the holy life as a genuine expression of our own personality, with needs and desires that are uniquely our own.

The passage of Scripture which develops most fully the concept of the church as the body of Christ (1 Corinthians 12) also emphasizes the unique contribution that each member makes to family life. If our approach to the holy life guarantees some flexibility for individual freedom, we have greater promise as a Christian family to become the people of God we ought to be. Family life requires commonality; it does not demand sameness. In fact, sameness would destroy the sense of the body. The unique diversity of all the members of the body is essential to the total working of the life of the church. The Spirit of God fashions individuals for particular roles, so that the body of Christ might have a full expression of the Christian life.

In a spiritual sense, God understands our need for a "given name" that fits us in a way that applies to no other Christian, and influences us in a manner similar to our family name of "Christian." It challenges each of us to be what God says, by way of promise, that we are. In Genesis 17:5 God changed the name of Abram to Abraham, which means "father of multitudes," before he and Sarah even had a son of their own. We know him today as Abraham because the rest of his life was directed toward the realization of God's promise signified by this personal name. The full scope of the promise lay beyond the vision of his own lifetime, but he believed God in every detail of it and rejoiced in every stage of its fulfillment.

The New Testament contains a similar account. Jesus met Simon, the son of John, and said his name should be Peter, "the rock" (John 1:42; cf. Matthew 16:18). While he showed great promise throughout Jesus' ministry, Peter certainly was not then "the rock." Yet, in the early church—witness the book of Acts, for example—he began to live up to the prophecy of his name.

For some of us, the stories of Abraham and Peter have a familiar ring because some particular spiritual experience has grasped us with a similar sense of God's call for us in life. For others, the sense of what we hope to be is less mystical, but nonetheless real. Out of a sober assessment of our God-given uniqueness, we aspire to be a particular kind of person or to fulfill a specific service for God's kingdom. Still others have seen a model of the Christian life in another Christian that acts like a magnet upon their own lives, drawing them on to fulfillment. Whatever the particular source of our inspiration may be, wherever the vision of the family name "Christian" comes into contact with our own unique quest for spiritual life, there we have discovered the identity of our individual, given name.

And this vision of a Christian future will mold and determine our life, for one of the dynamic realities of the Christian faith is that God's future can have greater control of our life than our past does. At times the promise of our given name seems like a distant dream—it portrays a person we hardly dare to believe we shall become. And we would flee from the implication of such a name except for the fact that it is God's name of promise for us. So like Abraham, we follow God's call to a land he will show us. And like Peter, we follow Christ till we are formed into the image of our Master. Like them we might fail—fail miserably. But God's promise draws us on till faith turns into sight, for with God nothing is impossible (Genesis 18:14; Mark 10:27).

Defining the holy life

What then is the holy life? It is the quest of the whole family of faith to grow up to the full significance of the name "Christian." It is, therefore, a group activity. In its teaching, worship, ministry, and discipline the Church is endeavoring to "present everyone perfect (complete, mature) in Christ" (Colossians 1:28). As a body (family) it is seeking to be the bride of Christ "as a radiant church, without stain or wrinkle or any other blemish, but holy and blameless" (Ephesians 5:27).

For the individual believer, the holy life defines the goal of his or her faith. It is to grow up in Christ, to become in every area of life a disciple of Jesus. Paul's expression of this desire is without parallel: "Not that I have already obtained all this, or have already been made perfect, but I press on to take hold of that for which Christ Jesus took hold of me" (Philippians 3:12). The grace of salvation has introduced us to life in Jesus Christ, and thereby laid claim to our allegiance to the life God has called us to. Realizing, acknowledging, and obeying this "upward call of God in Christ Jesus" (Philippians 3:14 RSV) are the essential ingredients of the holy life.

The holy life is both a celebration and a challenge. It celebrates the privilege of belonging to God's family, thankful for the grace which set us free from the life of sin. "How great is the love the Father has lavished on us, that we should be called children of God! And that is what we are!" (1 John 3:1). It is a challenge because we see possibilities to be like our Father who has made us his sons and daughters. "Dear friends, now we are children of God, and what we will be has not yet been made known. But we know that when he appears, we shall be like him, for we shall see him as he is. Everyone who has this hope in him purifies himself, just as he is pure" (1 John 3:2-3).

"Christian"—what mystery the name conceals and reveals!

Therefore, since we have a great high priest who has gone through the heavens, Jesus the Son of God, let us hold firmly to the faith we profess. For we do not have a high priest who is unable to sympathize with our weaknesses, but we have one who has been tempted in every way, just as we are—yet was without sin.

Hebrews 4:14-15

3

God Also Has a Name

Exodus 3:1-15; Hebrews 4:11-16

People become like the gods they worship. If their gods are fearsome spirits, they become people troubled by many fears. If their gods are immoral, like the Canaanite fertility deities, they fashion a society plagued by sexual immorality. If they worship warrior gods, like the Romans did Mars, they glorify warfare as the way to secure the interests of their government.

The opposite is also true. Those who know the God of the Bible to be merciful, holy, and loving will reflect lives characterized by peace, righteousness, and love. The key, then, to living well is to know the true God and to know him well. In other words, does God have a name? If so, what is it? For if one knows God's name, then he knows God, God's character, and God's will for mankind. In the biblical sense, this is what knowing God's name means.

One of the most significant accounts of the Old Testament is recorded in Exodus 3:1-15. Moses met God in the incident of the burning bush at Mt. Horeb (also called Sinai). Commissioned to deliver Israel from Pharaoh's bondage, Moses asked to know God's name. God's cryptic response was, "I am who I am." He then informed Moses that Israel henceforth, throughout all succeeding generations, should know him by the name Jehovah ("I Am"). What is so significant about this name? What did Moses learn about God through this disclosure of this name? How did it subsequently affect the people of God?

Jehovah is a holy God

Even before the disclosure of God's name, Moses was confronted with the holiness of God. He was curious about a bush that burned without being consumed. As yet he had no hint that the unusual spectacle was due to God's presence. Then the Lord called him by name and told him to come no nearer; in fact, Moses was to take off his sandals for he was standing on holy ground. When God revealed himself as the God of the patriarchs, Moses hid his face, fearful of looking upon God.

What was the point of this display of God's holiness? The essence of true worship is to know that God is unique. Beside him there is no other god (Exodus 20:2-3). The ancient world, as the modern world, was a department store filled with gods of every description. But only Jehovah was the true and living God (Jeremiah 10:10). This was demonstrated in the plagues of Egypt, each directed against one of the Egyptian deities. The gods of Egypt were impotent, but Jehovah delivered his people from the hand of Pharaoh.

People worship many gods because they feel no one god is adequate for all their needs. So they have one god of vegetation, another of flocks, and another for human needs. One is the god of love, another the god of childbirth, yet a third the god of death and the afterlife. The names and the descriptions are endless. The name "I Am" could never fit these gods; they all need something to complete the clause, like "I am the god of love." The name Jehovah ("I Am") stands in stark contrast; it is complete in itself, needing nothing else to complete the description. All the descriptive titles needed to depict other deities are already summed up in who God is. He is all the attributes associated with the multiplied gods in one, and that in absolute degree and total unity. There can be no other god beside him because there is no imperfection or lack of completion in him. God is! That is sufficient, for it says all that can be said.

God's holiness distinguishes him from other gods not only in his completeness but also in his consistency. His completeness manifests itself in uniform goodness. God does not have his off days, so to speak, in which he acts out of character with his name. God is not subject to dark moods and evil passions, leading him to change the rules of fellowship without notice from time to time. What a comfort it is to us to relate to the God who is reliable, a constant source of strength because his character, his actions, and his expectations are ever the same!

God's consistency means he does not hold us to a standard of conduct to which he himself does not adhere. The gods worshipped by the ancient Greeks were like this. They demanded honesty and chastity, for example. Yet the Greek legends about their gods are filled with stories of one god deceiving another god, and the Greek gods and goddesses were perpetually involved in illicit love affairs. It is little wonder that the Greeks of an enlightened age renounced their belief in such gods. We would renounce our belief in God, too, if he were like these pagan deities, for we know how much we dislike parents or rulers who impose rules upon us from which they exempt themselves. Jehovah, however, said, "Be holy because I, the Lord your God, am holy" (Leviticus 19:2). God's consistency wins our respect of his righteous law and our trust of his person. He is what he asks us to be.

Holiness, then, is not just one aspect of God's nature along with such other attributes as love, wisdom, or power. It is a word that depicts the sum total of God's being, that which separates him from all other gods. God is so truly in a class by himself that nothing else can be compared to him. When we hallow (sanctify, set apart) God's name (Matthew 6:9), we do far more than refuse to use it in profanity. It means that we acknowledge him as the only God, and give him devotion and recognition bestowed upon no one else or anything beside.

The holiness of God is thus synonymous with monotheism (the belief in one God). Israel struggled throughout the Old Testament with other gods in addition to Jehovah. It was not that they renounced the Lord. They failed to know him as the "I Am"; they sought in additional deities a completeness that they failed to realize in God alone. In the Sermon on the Mount, Jesus condemned those who tried to serve two masters—God and mammon (Matthew 6:19-24). The book of James indicted those Christians guilty of splitting their affection between God and worldly things. James called this double-mindedness "spiritual adultery" (See James 4:1-10). In other words, many religious people who professedly *believe* monotheism, actually *practice* polytheism (belief in many gods).

The holy life begins with the awareness of the great "I Am" God. It realizes that God alone is due our worship and our service. It makes God the focal point of our entire life, its involvements, and its relationships. It is the discipline of desire, lest we seek satisfaction (fulfillment) in that which is apart from God or contrary to him.

Moses' vision of God on Mt. Horeb became his point of orientation throughout the rest of his career. The same is true of the saints of all ages. Apart from this orientation we talk of Christian duties which fail to compel us, we speak of disciplines that fail to fashion us, we talk of love that does not constrain us, and offer a service which is not a labor of love. The first question of the holy life is not "how can I be holy?" Many ask that question and faithfully pursue the answers offered in response. But they are like those who run in place—going through the motions of running and exerting considerable energy. Yet there is no progress to show for the effort!

The primary question—and constant question—is, "who is the Lord God?" Above all else we must know God's name. All progress in the Christian life derives from our reverential worship of God, acknowledging him to be Lord of life and yielding to his rightful claim to our total life.

God's holiness in redemptive love

We have noted that the essence of God's holiness is his separateness from anyone or anything trying to lay claim to the title of god. But does not God's uniqueness also mean that he is "set apart from sinners" (Hebrews 7:26)? God told Moses to come no nearer to the bush and to put off his shoes—in Hebrew thought they were seen as defiled with the pollution of the earth—for he stood on holy ground. Moses hid his face, "afraid to look at God" (Exodus 3:6). Isaiah's vision of God in the temple produced a similar response. He cried, "Woe to me! . . . I am ruined! For I am a man of unclean lips, and I live among a people of unclean lips, and my eyes have seen the King, the Lord Almighty" (Isaiah 6:5). After the miraculous catch of fish impressed Peter that God was present in Christ, Peter fell down and said, "Go away from me, Lord; I am a sinful man!" (Luke 5:8).

We find this to be a natural reaction for humanity since the fall of Adam. When we confront the holiness of God, we are immediately aware of our sinfulness—our utter lack of fitness for fellowship with God. But God does not intend to reveal his holiness in order to accentuate the sense of distance between himself and us. In fact, God's sole purpose of the burning bush was to disclose to Moses his intention to *redeem* Israel from Egypt. The central quality of God's holiness, then, is his love—his desire to redeem men and women from the bondage to sin so that they might have perfect fellowship with God.

God's response to Isaiah and Peter is in keeping with this theme. God touched the lips of Isaiah, taking away his iniquity and making him a mouthpiece to Israel (Isaiah 6:6ff). God told Peter not to be afraid for henceforth he would catch men (Luke 5:10). God not only brought Moses, Isaiah, and Peter into intimate fellowship with himself, but he also made them instruments of redemption for their fellowmen.

God knows that we cannot cross the gulf between our sinfulness and his holiness. But that does not condemn us to continual distance and separation from God. However much our natural inclination is to shrink from the awesome holiness of God (see Hebrews 4:11-13), we need to wait before God till we know his compassionate, redemptive name. Thus, Hebrews 4:14-16 assures us, we can draw near to God because our high priest, Jesus, is sympathetic with our weakness and will bestow the mercy and grace we need. In Jesus (literally his name means "I Am Salvation"), the Infinite One bridges the gulf between God and man, takes away our sin, and makes us like himself. God's holiness in redemption conquers the separation sin created between God and humanity.

God's holiness in family intimacy

When Moses understood God's purpose to redeem Israel from Egypt, he felt compelled to ask the identity of God's name. It was then that God revealed his personal name Jehovah ("I Am"). He was the historic God of Moses' ancestors (Abraham, Isaac, and Jacob), but now he would be known by his personal covenant name. Through God's redemption of Israel from Egypt, a bond of intimacy between Jehovah and Israel would be established that could best be expressed in family terms. Henceforth God would refer to Israel as his wife or his son (Isaiah 54; the book of Hosea; Exodus 4:22-23; Jeremiah 31:20).

When Israel came out of Egypt, Moses led them to Sinai where God gave them the law (Exodus 19 and 20). This took place on the same mountain where God met Moses at the burning bush. God meant for the law to spell out the terms of the covenant, like the family rules that would regulate God's special relationship with the chosen people. Through the years, however, Israel seemed to lose sight of this personal side of the law. More and more it became an impersonal legal code that they were reluctant to obey. Eventually they took the name Jehovah ("I Am") and placed it upon a high pedestal of restraint. It was considered too sacred—too separated—to be pronounced, and they substituted another name (Adonai: Lord) for Jehovah whenever they encountered it in reading the Scripture. The personal, family sense of God's name was lost. Gone, too, was the intimate family context as the understanding of God's holiness. Now it was something remote, reserved only to God.

How necessary then for Jesus to come as Immanuel: "God with us!" Jesus transformed the righteous requirement of the law from a minus factor to a plus sign. Law ceases to feel like law when it is transformed into a child's obedience to the Father, for love converts law into the terms of family relationships.

Symbolic of all this was Jesus' reintroduction of God's personal name to his people. When Jesus prayed, he addressed God as "Abba, Father" (Mark 14:36). "Abba" was an intimate Aramaic word similar in meaning to "papa" or "daddy" in our tongue. Somehow this seems appropriate for Jesus. The amazing thing, however, is that the Spirit makes this intimate address for God the heart language of the Christian as well! (Romans 8:15; Galatians 4:6). Once again we feel the warmth of the Father's presence. His holiness is not a stern, remote demand for righteousness. Rather it is the intimacy of his love drawing us to himself, assuring us of our acceptance with him, and promising to make us like himself, pure in motive and conduct.

"Abba" in the New Testament recaptures the sense of family intimacy introduced by the name Jehovah in the Old Testament. It guards against our inclination to relate to God solely as the "God of our fathers." We need that sense of the historic acts of God. But if we stop there, God remains impersonal, and his holiness becomes remote. We then idolize saints of the past who knew God intimately and conclude that such a walk with God is not possible for us now. But in "Abba" he becomes our God in the here and now, and we feel the full promise of his name Jehovah. "I Am" means God's completeness is applied at the point of our needs. When Jehovah is our personal God, he cares for our needs like a parent cares for a child.

The promise of God's name

Frequently we approach the holy life in Christian settings with the words of Peter:

> As obedient children, do not conform to the evil desires you had when you lived in ignorance. But just as he who called you is holy, so be holy in all you do; for it is written: "Be holy, because I am holy" (1 Peter 1:14-16).

This demand for holy living is appropriate so long as we place it in its proper context. The previous chapter sought to do this in presenting the obligation to realize fully our Christian name. But our preaching is something less than the gospel (good news) if we do not do anything more than accentuate the demand of the holy life.

So many Christians seem to get mired down in a pattern of life that has more demands than it has promises. For many, the joy of salvation is lost in a bitter struggle to satisfy the "ought" of the Christian life. Some have surrendered themselves to despair, concluding that the holy life is something attained only by a few "athletes of the Spirit," but not available to the general run of believers. To Christians such as these, the promise of God's name is ecstatic good news. "You shall be holy" is as much a promise, guaranteed by God's own resources of redemptive love, as it is a demand. Only when we see God's personal resources placed at the point of our need does the slavish chain of "legal ought" fall from our hands and feet. We shout the "Abba" of God's children and know the Father will care for all our needs. The holy life will be ours, because it is his. We are his heirs, heirs of the promise. The knowledge of God's name—and all it stands for—is as a password to paradise.

You were taught, with regard to your former way of life, to put off your old self, which is being corrupted by its deceitful desires; to be made new in the attitude of your minds; and to put on the new self, created to be like God in true righteousness and holiness.

Ephesians 4:22-24

4

The Changing of Names

Genesis 32:22-32; Ephesians 4:17-24

The question was raised in our small group Bible study at the Miller's home on a rainy Sunday evening. "If Jacob had not deceived his brother, how could he ever have received the things God had promised to him? Don't we sometimes have to help out, so God's plan can be realized?" An interesting discussion followed, highlighted by current situations facing individuals and couples in our group.

In the course of the discussion it was pointed out that Jacob's deceptions had not really brought him what he sought. He had to leave everything he hoped to gain, because Esau intended to kill him. The wealth he finally possessed came through God's peculiar blessing, despite the attempts of his father-in-law to prevent that very outcome. Thus, the material blessing he sought came from God's hands, not from his own efforts. All that Jacob's deceptions accomplished was the complication of the process and the addition of unwelcomed pain for himself.

Just how do we obtain the promises of God—the promises inherent in our Christian name(s) and in God's name? Do we sit down and passively wait until God does it all? Do we rush in and try to give God a hand? Or is there a middle ground, a type of active faith which obediently follows the Lord in his pathway of blessing? Herein lies the clue to the development of the Christian life from babyhood to maturity. The story of Jacob gives us some very strong hints about the process.

Jacob—the revealing name

From the manner of his birth—as the second-born twin he clutched his brother Esau's heel—Jacob received his name of deceiver (supplanter: one who takes by the heel). He proved the predictive aptness of this name on two occasions. First, he seized upon his brother's hunger to get him to "sell his birthright." Then, with the help of his conniving mother, he deceived his father into giving him the blessing intended for Esau. Jacob seems to have done these things with little or no remorse for his deeds or the people they injured.

Several factors changed his point of view. First, Jacob was driven from the very things he thought he won, when he had to flee from Esau's wrath. Then, he experienced "poetic justice" in an uncle who was as deceptive as he had been. Twice his uncle Laban deceived him: in the daughter he gave Jacob as wife and in the malicious changes in his wages. Lastly, when he wished to return to his father's inheritance promised to him, Jacob's very deeds of deception stood in his way. Unless his injured brother Esau was agreeable, there was no human way to receive what was promised to him.

Jacob now realized the full implications of his name. Though a son of the promise, his deceptive character was standing in the way of realizing the promise. It was not in his power to undo the damage he had done nor to change his name. (Keep in mind that, biblically, names revealed one's nature or character.) Jacob was in a pinch where he could neither go backward nor forward. Behind him was Laban, his father-in-law, who would claim all his possessions if Jacob returned to Laban's territory. Before him was Esau and four hundred men, blocking his way to that which God had promised him.

Jacob's only refuge was prayer (Genesis 32:9-12). He prayed to the God who had blessed him in the past. He recalled the promises of God and God's command to return to his own country. He pleaded with God to deliver him from Esau whom he feared. And through a long and lonely night, he wrestled with a heavenly protagonist. In the course of the struggle, his angelic visitor touched Jacob's thigh, crippling him in such a way that he could never be a warrior. Still Jacob clung to his host, refusing to let him go unless he would bless him. Finally, the messenger asked for his name. And he said, "Jacob." It was the supreme confession! It was the acknowledgement of what he was, a deceiver. This was the heart of the issue, for it was this—not Esau—that kept Jacob from God's blessing.

Genesis 32, Jacob's confession, is the counterpart to Exodus 3, the disclosure of God's name to Moses. If we are to know God by his intimate name, we must be willing to confess to him our intimate name. This is confession at the deepest level, for we must confess before God the worst about ourselves. It is a confession that leaves us wounded, incapable of any defense, completely vulnerable before the Lord. So helpless are we that all we can do is cling in desperation to the Lord, imploring him to bless us, lest we perish without inheriting his promises.

Israel—the name of blessing

Jacob's confession—of all that he had been and was—became his door to blessedness. Immediately God said, "Your name will no longer be Jacob, but Israel, because you have struggled with God and with men and have overcome" (Genesis 32:28). God had taken away the reproach of his former name and all that it implied. Instead, he received the name by which all his descendants would be known. His new name implied that he had inherited the promises God had made to him earlier (Genesis 28:10-22) in the famous dream of the ladder between heaven and earth. Those promises were that Jacob would inherit the land of Canaan and that his descendants would be without number. The full extent of the promises would be centuries in fulfillment, but soon thereafter Jacob possessed a token portion of the land (Genesis 33:18-19). And the twelve sons, by which the tribes of his descendants would be known, reached completion in the birth of Benjamin (Genesis 35:16-18).

For Jacob, the central issue of his blessing was that he had come to know God "face to face" (Genesis 32:30). This is why he called the place of his night-wrestling Peniel ("the face of God"). For the Hebrew people, to know God "face to face" meant an intimate relationship that few enjoyed. (See, for example, Deuteronomy 34:10, which refers to Moses, "whom the Lord knew face to face.") It was this vision of God, this relationship, that transformed Jacob's life and character. The Jacob narratives before Peniel and after Peniel read differently. Before Jacob knew God intimately, he was aggressively self-seeking, abrasive, and exhibited little devotion to God. After Peniel, he was satisfied with what God had given him, conciliatory in human relationships (note his meeting with Esau— Genesis 33), and full of worship toward God (note Genesis 33:20; 35:1-15; 46:1-4).

The development of the holy life is dependent upon an intimate relationship with God, for apart from this there is little development in Christlike character. A close walk with God benefits us in many ways. An awareness of God's presence helps us to understand ourselves better and realize the areas where we most need his help. An intimate walk with God stimulates a desire to live pleasing to God in all things. It also enables us to believe that the

God of miracles can change people as well as things. It was said of Moses that "he persevered because he saw him who is invisible" (Hebrews 11:27). Christians who become mature in Christ are those who have come to know God in this "face to face" fashion. There is a God-consciousness about them that pervades their whole life. They are not mere bumper-sticker Christians. Rather, one senses that the Christlike character reflected in them is due to their persistent cultivation of God's presence in their lives.

Can God change my name, too?

There is little doubt that what happened to Jacob at Peniel was a dramatic event. The question for us, however, is how to apply this lesson to our own case. There are those who write off all biblical stories as unique to that age, as something that cannot possibly happen to a modern follower of Christ. But this approach misses the point of Hebrews 11, where numerous examples of those who walked in obedience to God—including Jacob—are given as illustrations of the life of faith to which God calls us today (Hebrews 12:1-2).

However, there is also danger in an opposite error. Some try to duplicate the exact experiences of biblical characters. They are reluctant to claim any activity of God in their lives simply because their experience is not as dramatic as a particular character in a biblical event. The error here is the failure to realize that God deals differently with each individual personality. The Bible characters themselves have different stories, because God met the needs unique to them and their individual circumstances. God's grace is unchanging; all may experience it. But individuals will encounter that grace in as many different ways as their needs require.

The Jacob story highlights two closely related truths that we need to grasp in approaching the holy life. First, as illustrated in Jacob's change of name, God does change people's characters. Secondly, an intimate relationship with God is the key to the development of the holy life. If we can bring those truths home to our own Christian lives, we too will be blessed by the account of Jacob at Peniel.

From Adam to Christ

Why would a Christian be interested in a change of name (meaning a change of character)? Certainly no fault can be found with such noble terms as believer, disciple, or Christian. The problem, however, is not to be found with the names salvation brings to us. The problem has to do with our pre-Christian name and the "hang-over effect" it has on our Christian life.

Ephesians 4:22-24 will help us get the situation in focus:

> You were taught, with regard to your former ways of life, to put off your *old self*, which is being corrupted by its deceitful desires; to be made new in the attitude of your minds; and to put on the *new self*, created to be like God in true right-eousness and holiness.

In the original language Paul used in writing this passage, the underlined words were "old man" and "new man." What did he mean by those expressions? Much of Paul's thinking divides human experience into two spheres of influence—that of Adam (old man) and that of Christ (new man). One can see the clearest expression of this "two sphere" aspect in such passages as Romans 5:6-21 and 1 Corinthians 15:20-50 (especially verses 22 and 45-47). Before Christ and outside of Christ, every human being is under the influence of Adam (and all that his name implies about sin and its consequences). Those in Christ go by his name (and all that it implies in salvation from sin and its consequences). Since the Adam story of Genesis precedes the Christ event of the Gospels, Paul uses the names "old man" and "new man" as code names for these diverse realities.

"Well," one might respond, "did we not pass from the 'old man' (Adam) to the 'new man' (Christ) at conversion?" Does not the Scripture say in obvious Adam-Christ symbols, "if anyone is in Christ, he is a new creation; the old has gone, the new has come!" (2 Corinthians 5:17)? A straightforward response is both "yes" and "no." There are times that Paul gathers together all the diverse aspects of salvation and speaks of them as a single unit, much as we would sometimes talk of life as a unified whole. At other times he concentrates on separate aspects (or stages) of salvation, just as we separate life into diverse periods and components. One illustration of this is Paul's discussion of the resurrection from the dead. While life in Christ guarantees it, no one experiences it at the same moment as conversion. Thus, the sons of God eagerly await this final benefit of salvation (Romans 8:23).

We might borrow an illustration from physical life and apply it to the discussion at hand. In a newborn baby there is all the potential of life. All subsequent stages of life lie coded within the infant's physical composition—like so many packages within a package, awaiting the appropriate time of their unwrapping. Thus, in a sense, all of life lies within the miracle of birth—all that one will be is already there in undeveloped form. On the other hand, life is measured out in units and stages of development. Growth can be interrupted or retarded at any stage, frustrating the potential promised by birth.

Now, in terms of the Christian life—especially as Paul portrays it—conversion introduces us into the totally new realm of salvation in all its aspects. But not everything that belongs to the "new man" is put on instantaneously. The crucial thing is that we have been rescued from the old life (with its threatening consequences) into the sphere of salvation (and all its promises of fulfillment). Conversion, as the boundary point between these spheres, is thus a glorious miracle; it guarantees new life though it does not fulfill it.

What we are talking about is like the dawning of a new day. When the sun rises, we have visible proof that night is gone and day has arrived. Yet there are still traces of the night, for it is not yet as light as it will be at noonday. The chill of the night may remain for a while longer, and the dew that settled during the darkness may yet make the grass wet. The Christian life is like that. Traces of the "old man" (Adam) remain in spite of the clear evidence that a new day in Christ has begun.

Many, if not all, Christians realize this to be true in their life. They discover, according to Galatians 5:16-17, that the desires of the "old man" ("flesh" in RSV; "sinful nature" in NIV) conflict with the mind of the Spirit (which is the controlling aspect of the "new man" in Christ). Some habits of speech and conduct from their former life in sin may persist in the early stages of their Christian life. Much more distressing is the fact that patterns of thought (imagination, desires, attitudes, and view of life) which are not at all Christian disrupt their endeavors to obediently follow the example Jesus set for his disciples. Alas, Adam is a fierce contestant! One does not easily shake off his name (his influence).

At this point Paul's teaching in Ephesians 4:22-24 comes in. The Apostle does not view the situation as hopeless. We Christians can do something about changing our names! Wherever and whenever a manifestation of the "old man" (whether thought or conduct) is discovered, we are instructed to put it off. We are not to go on as if it does not matter that we are influenced by the "old man" in this area of life. Neither are we to throw up our hands in fatalistic despair, saying, "I've always been this way, and I cannot change now." Jacob might well have said the same about his deceitful nature before Peniel. Here, as elsewhere, faith is the key to victory. For God is not so unjust as to command us to put off the "old man" and then make no provision for it to be accomplished.

Every command of the gospel implies the promise of God's grace. To the lame man at the Pool of Bethsaida Jesus said, "Get up! Pick up your mat and walk" (John 5:8). Now the man could have objected to this command in light of his inability to walk. He might have become angry and said, "Jesus, that is not a fair command. You are telling me to do the one thing I have been unable to do for thirty-eight years." But he did not. Knowing full well his own impotence, he sensed in Jesus' command a promise of help. When he made the effort to rise, he found God gave strength to his disabled legs. If Christians would put just half the effort into obeying the gospel command to "put off the old man" that they spend justifying the shadow of Adam over their lives, the world would be amazed at the change that came over the church.

It is said that "nature abhors a vacuum." This is certainly true in the spiritual realm. We cannot permanently dislodge old patterns of thought and behavior unless we replace them with proper thoughts and conduct. In Bible study and meditation, in prayer and fasting, in worship and service, and in fellowship with other Christians, we learn to think God's thoughts after him and to imitate the ways of Christ. Sin does not spring from such a soil, and evil cannot grow on this food. Pack life full of the knowledge of God, and his likeness will appear in due course. And so Paul commands us "to put on the new man."

For me the most interesting part of a sandwich is

what lies between the two pieces of bread. Sandwiched between Paul's two commands—"put off the old man" and "put on the new man"—is this meaty injunction: "and be made new [renewed] in the attitude of your minds." Even if you do not like English grammar, notice the verb: "be made new." Scripture does not say, "renew the spirit of your mind," as if it is something we can do by ourselves. Rather it suggests that the crucial renewal of our inner being must come from God the Spirit. For in the Ephesian epistle it is the Spirit who enlightens our minds with the possibilities of divine grace (1:16-23) and fills us with inner strength beyond our own possibilities (3:14-21). It is in the Holy Spirit that we discover how God changes our name.

The breath of life

Genesis 2:7 says God breathed life into the nostrils of Adam and he became a living soul. Sin corrupted and destroyed the life God gave Adam. In Christ the creative breath of God was given anew to mankind. In this new creation (2 Corinthians 5:17) the old passes away and the new image of man as he should be—Jesus Christ—appears. When those of us who are called Christian mourn the fact that Adam's name (nature) still haunts us, we need to be *renewed* in the spirit of our minds. The breath of God's spirit can fill our vessel of clay until all acknowledge that "this all-surpassing power is from God and not from us" (2 Corinthians 4:7).

Unless God breathes life into our soul, we are as helpless as Adam on the ground—a human form, but lacking life. Unless God changes our name (nature/character), we will continue to be the Jacob we despise and never become the Israel we aspire to be. Unless God provides the vital strength, we are as impotent as the poolside man; we can neither "put off the old man" nor "put on the new man." But God's great design is " to renew us in the spirit of our minds." He is the God who makes possible the changing of names. That's why he comes to us and says, "Christian, do you want to be made whole? If so, rise, take up your mat, and walk." He who discerns the face of the Master will see there the answer to his incredulous heart. God asks not that we do the impossible. God asks us to trust him to work the impossible in us. The real question is "do I believe that Jesus, the Lord and Giver of life, can change my name?" Faith believes the promises of God are not in vain; God will renew my inner being till my name is Israel, too.

Do not conform any longer to the pattern of this world, but be transformed by the renewing of your mind. Then you will be able to test and approve what God's will is—his good, pleasing and perfect will.

Romans 12:2

5

Living For What Matters Most

Matthew 6:19-34; Romans 12:1-8

It is not at all uncommon to hear one of my preschool sons giving some sort of frustrated utterance at the impossibility of managing two tasks at once. Often it is a matter of trying to lift two objects at once—either one of which he could manage, but the combined bulk being more than his store of strength. Again, he will try to carry several objects through an opening which is not large enough for them all at once, though it would permit one to pass at a time. The parent's task in those situations is to convince him that a reduction in load will make transit possible.

If all of us could master those lessons in childhood, our adult experience would be considerably more successful. But, alas, we don't seem to transpose these lessons into adult situations! The grasping, self-centered human spirit seems intent on multiple pleasures, accumulating many things, and devouring life like a glutton at a picnic. Thus our lives are overwrought with care and burdened with activity. Enough never seems to be enough. We have made ourselves slaves to multiple masters, each demanding his full service or extracting a pound of flesh as compensation.

We do well to remind ourselves that the great sin of the Old Testament was not idolatry *per se*, but syncretism: the worship of Jehovah *along with* several other popular deities of the surrounding culture. The prophets of Israel tried to recall the people to a true monotheism, reminding them that Jehovah was "a jealous God" who would not share his honor with any other. The prophets called Israel to consecration, the dedication of themselves to Jehovah to work out his will in all of life.

The holy life is a call to the same type of consecration that the prophets of old demanded of God's people. On the one hand, it is a call to those who labor and are overburdened with the care of many things. It promises rest in the yoke of Christ, for Christ's service does not overtax human strength nor overburden the human spirit (Matthew 11:28-30). The essence of the "simple life" is the reduction of life's masters to one. On the other hand, it is a call to serve the Lord in the fullness of heart and life, to devote all of life's energies and resources to the only Master who is called Good.

The problem of "double vision"

Some of us are old enough to remember the pleasures afforded by the stereoscope. Whole afternoons could be enlivened by viewing pictures with this marvelous invention. It made use of two optical lenses and picture cards with two photos of the same object taken from different points. The net result was an impression of depth—a picture in three dimensions.

Imagine, however, the confusion in sight that would result if two entirely different pictures were viewed at the same time, a different image for each eye. Prolonged exposure to such distorted vision would produce headaches at the very least, if not more serious visual distortion which, at its most severe stage, could cause a loss of equilibrium.

One of the greatest problems for those who would be Christian is just such distortion of vision. With one eye on the Lord, the other eye focuses upon another master, or a whole sequence of masters at different moments. Common among these other masters are materialism (Matthew 6:19-34), worldliness (1 John 2:15-17), or a particular besetting sin (Hebrews 12:1).

The consequences are varied, and the tragic examples are myriad. This is why a host of believers cease to grow. In the parable of the soils, Jesus explained the seed among the thorns as those who "are choked by life's worries, riches and pleasures" (Luke 8:14). Many are so influenced by secular culture (worldliness) that they frequently oppose the work of God without realizing their error. Satan must surely rejoice when Christians become his agents and "plead Baal's cause" (Judges 6:31). Other believers dissipate their spiritual resources in besetting sins, often bringing dishonor to Christ's name and the church which proclaims it.

Where such conditions prevail, one finds the "lukewarm" Christianity so detestable to God (Revelation 3:16-17). Here will be found professed believers less zealous for God than they were in the first moments of their Christian life (Revelation 2:4). From such a seedbed will come quarrels and fightings among Christians (1 Corinthians 6:1-8; James 4:1-4). Generally one will also find weakness in the devotional life, halfhearted and perfunctory worship, grudging stewardship, and little or no witnessing. Here, too, will be discovered the worst form of legalism: Christians whose aim is to meet the most minimal requirements of God's law. They seem intent on seeing how close they can walk near the precipice of evil without actually slipping over the edge. While these worst of symptoms may not appear in every case of "double-vision" believers, the general lack of spiritual growth and the absence of an appetite for the things of God are the telltale signs of the malady nonetheless.

Hallowing God's name

The need for a single focus in life would seem to be obvious. Immediately, however, the question arises about what that focus could be. Is there any being which has the intrinsic right to claim my absolute allegiance? Is there any cause worthy enough for me to devote myself and my resources to it without reservation? Unless we can answer these questions affirmatively, it is not likely that we will consecrate ourselves to the Lord. Consecration requires a recognition of the God whose servant I am and the type service appropriate to him.

The opening words of the Lord's Prayer are helpful at this point. They read:

Our Father in heaven,
hallowed be your name,
your kingdom come,
your will be done
on earth as it is in heaven.
(Matthew 6:9-10)

God has revealed himself by the intimate name of Father. While this implies a father's concern for all our needs (including daily bread, verse 11), it becomes most meaningful in terms of salvation. We who had been prodigals, squandering our Father's inheritance, have been welcomed back to his fellowship with full rights of sonship through the redemptive sacrifice of Christ (Luke 15:11-32). With joy and wonder we receive his mercy and grace by acknowledging him as our Father (Romans 8:15). For those who have experienced redemption, there is always a debt of love to the Father. There is an awareness that "we are not our own, for we were bought with the price" of Christ's blood (See 1 Corinthians 6:19-20; 1 Peter 1:18-20). Consecration, then, is a service of gratitude to one whose love can never be repaid. In fact, true consecration does not think in terms of measures and limits of love. (Such cold legalistic reasoning does not merit the term love.) It is love answering to love—loving God because he first loved us (1 John 4:19).

One always senses certain commitments to parents that he feels to no one else. But God as Father is in a class by himself. He is to be compared to none other, for there is no rival that is his equal. There is but one God, and all other things owe their existence to him. We dare not think of God's claims upon us as of no more intrinsic worth than those of other claims upon us. To waver in our allegiance between God and materialism is to be guilty of profaning his name in the most blatant way. For in doing so we are counting God as common, worthy of no more attention and respect than food and shelter or real estate and stocks. To hallow God's name means much more than refraining from profanity in our speech. It means realizing God is in a class by himself so that we regard nothing else as having the kind of claim upon our affections and loyalties as he does. Consecration, then is the hallowing of God's name in all of life. It means that the choices of life are made from the perspective of God's kingdom. It makes "Thy will be done" the highest priority in life.

Many Christians are continually profaning God's name by refusing to acknowledge his lordship over their entire lives. No wonder so few seem to inherit the full blessings of salvation. Before Israel entered into Canaan they were to consecrate (the biblical word translated sanctify in KJV and RSV) themselves and prepare to follow the ark of the "Lord of all the earth" (Joshua 3:5, 11, 13). Everything won in battle was to be dedicated to the Lord. Achan, however, saw some things he wanted for himself and consequently was cut off from the promised land (Joshua 7). Many others compromised with the pagan inhabitants of Palestine and also lost their inheritance.

(Note the Book of Judges.) Finally, the nation as a whole was driven into exile from the promised land because they failed to dedicate themselves exclusively to the ways of Jehovah.

The exact opposite of Israel was the example of Jesus Christ. From the manger to the cross, his constant motto was "Thy will be done!" (See Hebrews 10:7) His use of time and his relation to material comforts were determined by his commitment to fulfill the Father's works. He did not even consider his life as his own, but he laid it down in order to accomplish the Father's will. Nor did he object to the shame and suffering which accompanied his death, as if the Father was requiring some unreasonable act on his part. Difficult as the experience of the cross was, he consented to the will of his Father. In his pattern of obedience, Jesus set the example of true consecration. Here, as in all things, we are called to imitate his example.

The content of consecration

Granted that God is deserving the full consecration of our lives, what principles guide the manner of consecration acceptable to God? Three aspects seem worthy of consideration.

First, life as a whole must be consecrated to God. One of the great temptations for the Christian is to divide life into sacred and secular compartments. God's rule is acknowledged in the former area, but exempted from the latter. There is something of the feeling that, having paid our dues in certain religious categories, we are entitled to run other aspects of life according to personal desires. For example, some feel that the observance of the Lord's day is a sufficient acknowledgment of God's lordship over time; the other six days of the week are strictly their own affair. Again, many feel that giving their tithe fulfills the obligation of the stewardship of resources. How they earn their income (their business ethics) or how they spend what remains after tithes and taxes doesn't seem to them to be a spiritual issue. By the same sort of reasoning they manage to exclude God from questions of leisure activities and a host of other issues in life.

As the Old Testament law addressed every area of life, so also the New Testament directs us to do everything to the glory of God (Colossians 3:17). If we note the apostolic injunctions to godly living, we will discover something of a set pattern that includes civic responsibilities, family relationships, work and economic concerns, and church life (Ephesians 4:21-6:9; Colossians 3:18-4:6; 1 Peter 2:11-3:8). The lordship of Christ was extended to all areas of life.

Down through the centuries of the Christian faith, the Christians who were exemplary were those who understood consecration as involving all of life. This was true of the monastic movement at its best. It was also true of the Anabaptists, the Puritans, the Pietists, the early Methodists, and many others. In fact, wherever the church has experienced a revival of biblical Christianity, this understanding of total consecration has always come into focus.

Secondly, consecration means that kingdom values take priority over other concerns. In Matthew 6 Jesus recognized that humans need food, clothing, and shelter, but he placed a higher value upon the kingdom of God and the righteousness belonging to it. Comfort needs are not the ultimate issues in life; meaning and purpose in life are not to be found in them. One should not seek these things by any means and at all costs. The same holds true of many other things which the Gentiles (here used in the sense of the ungodly) seek—wealth, power, popularity, and all that belongs to the so-called "good life."

Consecration, in this sense, affects many practical

decisions in life. One would resist the offer of a college education at government expense in exchange for military service, because the biblical values of love and respect for God-given life are ultimate concerns, while an academic degree is not. Vocational choices would also be made with the kingdom in view. There are jobs that pay well which no Christian in good conscience could hold. In regard to the day of worship, one might refuse a job requiring work on Sunday and take another one which makes regular church participation possible. In regard to the important area of Christian family life, one might avoid jobs which keep him from home too much. Many Christian families ought to resist full-time employment of both parents. The souls of our children are a kingdom priority, but many are sacrificing their children on the pagan altar of materialism.

Kingdom values call us as Christians to the simple lifestyle. As followers of the lowly Nazarene who carried his entire wardrobe on his person, had no home to call his own, and rarely enjoyed even the travel convenience of a donkey, how dare we invest thousands of dollars in clothing, live in palatial homes, and cram our driveways with expensive cars? It might be true that our income makes such things possible, but that is sub-Christian ethics. While people starve, shiver in the cold, and die from diseases that can be prevented, we can never be consecrated to God's kingdom above all else and live in such selfish indulgence.

If the spirit of consecration to kingdom values were to flourish, then many would follow the example of C. T. Studd, missionary to three different continents. When this popular cricket player in England was converted in a D. L. Moody evangelistic campaign, he not only gave up his athletic career; he also gave away his vast family inheritance lest it hinder him from following God's call upon his life. Others would imitate John Wesley, who believed that

God's blessing in material things was designed to make you a benefactor of the needy. Having learned what it took to live frugally, he lived on that amount year after year. Instead of improving his living standard as his income increased, he took the opportunity to give away more each year. I commend the example of Jess and Ruth Stoner, who obeyed God's call to sell their suburban home and move into the city of Harrisburg, Pennsylvania, in order to identify with a congregation seeking to minister in the inner city context. With the great need for an evangelical witness in the city, others need to follow the Stoners' ordering of kingdom values.

Thirdly, consecration involves giving ourselves as "living sacrifices" (Romans 12:1-2). God is interested in the surrender of *our selves* to him more than the things which we consecrate to his use. King David of old learned that it was not burnt offerings and sacrifices that God required. Rather, God delighted in a spirit of brokenness and contriteness of heart (Psalm 51:16-17). For if our hearts are captive to the lordship of Christ, then the total resources of our lives are at God's disposal as well. God does not want our service to be forced from us, like the reluctant compliance one could get by threatening a slave with punishment. Our obedience is to be that of sons and daughters who are motivated by love for the Father.

The lack of true consecration is manifested in reluctant, tardy, and intermittent obedience. There is a human reluctance to make long-term commitments to another. We are afraid of another getting control of our innermost being. We want to reserve for ourselves veto power over all decisions. We want to bargain our obedience and measure out our service, especially if costly sacrifice is involved. When Jesus stands across our pathway and says, "Follow me," we find it frightening to make an open-ended commitment to follow. It is not just a question of putting a five dollar bill into the offering plate or giving a week of my time to help the victims of a natural disaster. It is signing over the rights of my life to God for all of the unknown future—a sacrifice of my whole life. It means that I renounce my selfish claim to control the destiny of my life and accept Jesus as my master. It is to bring the will of God from the margin of my life to the center of it. Jesus said the issues of life flow out of the heart (Matthew 12:33-37; cf. Proverbs 4:23). Our lives will never be true living sacrifices until Christ is Lord over our innermost self. Consecration plainly involves the cross—the death to the natural (self-centered) approach to life—and the resurrection to the Christ-centered way of living.

Yet for all this, our fears of consecration are frequently unfounded. We have never found another human that we could trust to be absolute lord over our very being. We project our image of others onto God and fear that he will be a despotic master, ordering us to do things we would rather not do, just to prove his right to our complete obedience. At least that was a very real fear in my life for a time. I feared that what I enjoyed doing, God would certainly ask me to forgo, while whatever seemed like a fearsome task would certainly become a divine requirement. It is not hard to imagine how such perceptions of God make consecration a difficult issue.

The consecration God calls us to, however, is to be a "living" sacrifice. It fits the aptitudes and interests we have in life. It is in keeping with our individual personalities. Thus, as we read on in Romans 12 (verses 3-8), we notice that the service we are to render to God is in keeping with God-given gifts, whether prophecy, teaching, financial contributions, or the care of the needy. God does not intend to fit us into unnatural modes of service which would destroy our spirit and make life a dreary affair. Instead, God seeks the freeing up of our personalities so we may enjoy doing God's will as the "good and acceptable and perfect" way to live (Romans 12:2 RSV).

Is consecration an act or an attitude?

Some talk of consecration as a definite spiritual experience when they surrendered themselves to God's will for their lives. Others see consecration as an attitude that expresses itself in repeated decisions to do God's will in their life. Which is right? Actually, both are correct. Consecration is in this respect much like marriage. There comes a moment in a relationship when two people are willing to formally bind themselves to the will of the other. Yet that commitment will be fleshed out in the countless situations of life requiring new and deeper commitments to each other. The two aspects of commitment complement each other.

Consecration in the spiritual realm is the same. It is a definite act in that, somewhere in a person's Christian pilgrimage, there must be the definite commitment to the claims of Christ as Lord. One does not know what all that will mean in the indeterminate future, but it is a predetermination of the heart to follow God's will, however he directs.

In places where Christians are persecuted, the tendency of converts is to make such commitments from the beginning of their Christian life. Where one finds the phenomenon of childhood conversions, or where the cultural pressures are conducive to Christian professions of faith, there is less of this understanding of consecration at the initial stages of Christian experience. When these converts reach adolesence (either physically or spiritually defined), they tend to wrestle with the sharply focused demands of discipleship. Many of them experience a meaningful act of consecration at that point, in which they accept the full responsibility to be a disciple of Jesus Christ.

Beyond the decisive act of consecration, however, there is a constant dimension to consecration in the entirety of the Christian life. Experience deepens one's commitment to the Lord and brings increasing stability to one's discipleship. Increased knowledge of God's will for his people requires that we extend the limits of consecration to include new steps of obedience. Certain situations requires us to suffer with and for our Lord; again our commitment must stretch to say, "Lord, even in this, thy will be done." Our resources might increase, and our sense of stewardship must grow with it. Our vocational roles may change, bringing greater influence to our lives; we will need to have increased carefulness that God would fashion that influence for good.

Both in the initial commitment to discipleship and in the constant attitude that must characterize it, consecration is that acknowledgement that only one Name deserves to be the center of our life. Only the God of Calvary, who gave us his all, has the right to ask in return that we give him our all. God, alone, is a cause sufficient for the investment of one's entire life. Consecration writes the name of God over all of life and says, "Amen!"

But the Counselor, the Holy Spirit, whom the Father will send in my name, will teach you all things and will remind you of everything I have said to you.

John 14:26

6

The Personal Ministry
of the Holy Spirit

John 14:15-29; Acts 1:4-8; 2:1-4

When Jesus told his disciples that he was about to
return to the Father, they virtually went into shock. God
had come to them in human form, and they had lived a few
years of life in a dimension of reality that had escaped
mankind for centuries. They could not comprehend how
they could ever live "normal" lives again, if the very center
of life were suddenly taken from them. They would be
spiritual orphans, with a sense of loss more profound than
the loss of an earthly parent.

It was then that Jesus began to talk to them about
another *parakletos* (Comforter, Counselor, Advocate), the
Holy Spirit, whom he would send to them. This Comforter or Counselor would be to them what Jesus had been in
the days of his earthly ministry. In fact, he would be the
very Spirit of Christ, making Christ as real to the disciples
as when he was among them, even though they could no
longer see him with their physical eyes. When the Spirit
came upon them they would no longer feel like orphans,
but they would know their relationship with the Father
through Jesus the Son. Pentecost verified Jesus' promise of
a Comforter. As the rushing wind of that day filled all the

house, so also the presence of the Spirit filled the empty recesses of the disciples' hearts. Again they knew that God was with them, the source and strength of life.

The teaching of Jesus (John 14) and the experience of the disciples (Acts 1 and 2) highlight two broad categories of the personal ministry of the Holy Spirit. First, there is the ministry of the Spirit in and for the believer. Then, there is the ministry of the Spirit through the believer for the sake of the world. These two focal points shape the content of the dicussion in this chapter.

The Spirit's ministry to believers

Before Jesus spoke to his disciples of what the Spirit would do, he first called their attention to the divine personhood of the Spirit. The literal meaning of the word translated "Counselor" is "one called to the side of." Except for necessary times of retreat or reflection, we do not like to be alone. We are made for companionship. We appreciate the relationship of someone being present with us, even if not much is being said and little else is being done for us. The Holy Spirit is God's companionship with us. Apart from what he does in our lives, the fact of his personal presence brings a sense of rightness, of completeness, in our relationship with God. In the Holy Spirit we relate to God on a "first name" basis.

Often we fail to realize the implication of Jesus' reference to the Spirit as *"another* Counselor." The word "another" in the original language means "another of the same kind." In other words, our best clue to the person and ministry of the Spirit is the person and ministry of Jesus. A lot of distorted views could be avoided if people could think of the Spirit as being like Christ. The Holy Spirit is not some mysterious force or influence which is going to take over our faculties, like a cosmic hypnotist, and make us do a lot of weird things we would not choose to do under our own control. Quite the opposite, the Spirit will interact with us gently and winsomely, just like Jesus treated people when he walked among them.

Further proof that the Spirit is like Jesus is seen in his ministry to believers. He carries on the same activities now as Jesus did for the disciples during his ministry.

Ministry of teaching

Teaching was so much a part of Jesus' ministry that people often addressed him simply as "Teacher." Jesus taught by word (often in story form), by example, and by "hands-on" experiences for his disciples. The Spirit, he said, would continue to do this for his followers. He would be known as the Spirit of truth because he would bring to mind the things Jesus taught (John 14:17, 26). The Spirit would guide into all truth, including necessary knowledge of things yet to come (John 16:13). His "anointing" would keep Christians from being carried away by doctrinal error (1 John 2:18-27). In short, whenever the Word would be read or proclaimed, the Spirit would enlighten its truth and inspire its effect.

The greatest way to remember something is to find some way to associate it with your own life. Thus the Holy Spirit takes the truth of the Word and applies it to some immediate need of our life. Do we lack understanding? The Holy Spirit illuminates so we might form our thinking correctly. Do we take spiritual things for granted? Then he inspires the truth, kindling new excitement in our heart for the things of God. Are we weak and spiritually mal-nourished? The Spirit makes the truth meat and bread to us, giving us strength to live. Do we have a decision to make? He will bring a passage to our attention that shows us the way to go. The same Spirit who told the biblical writers what to say is the teacher/interpreter of Christians today, so we can understand the message God has given.

Ministry in prayer

Jesus' disciples once asked him to teach them to pray. His immediate response was to give them the model prayer we call the Lord's prayer (Matthew 6:9-12). But he did much more. He gave them his own life as a model of effective prayer. He taught them that attitudes were more important than the words that were spoken or the length of the prayers (Matthew 6:5-15). He taught them to be persistent in prayer (Luke 18:1-8) and to pray in faith, confident that the Father knew their needs and was eager to meet them (Luke 11:1-13). He showed them the power in prayer when it reaches such depths of expression as "not my will but thine be done," and "Father, forgive them, they don't know what they are doing" (See Matthew 26:39-42 and Luke 23:34).

In like manner the Spirit vitalizes our prayer life. Perhaps the best commentary on what it means to pray "in the Spirit" is provided by Romans 8:26-27:

> In the same way, the Spirit helps us in our weakness. We do not know what we ought to pray, but the Spirit himself intercedes for us with groans that words cannot express. And he who searches our hearts knows the mind of the Spirit, because the Spirit intercedes for the saints in accordance with God's will.

The Spirit is the one who stands between the Father and his will for us and the needs of our heart, however poorly we understand or express them in prayer. He makes prayer more than just a pious exercise or a religious monologue. Instead, the Spirit helps us experience prayer as Jesus did: a genuine dialogue and an intimate communion with the Father.

Ministry against sin

In the course of his ministry, Jesus was not silent about sin and its effects. His teaching, however, pointed to the real root of sin as a condition of the heart. It was the things within, Jesus said, that corrupted people's lives and produced the outward deeds of evil. By the transparent goodness of his life, Jesus brought condemnation to those whose motivations were not wholesome. Above all, Jesus delighted in speaking the word which freed people from sin. The literal meaning of the Greek word for "forgive" is "to send away, to dismiss." Jesus had power over the guilty memory of sin, the powerful hold sin had upon people's lives, and dreadful consequences it produced.

It is not surprising, then, that another ministry of the Spirit that Jesus explained to his disciples was in regard to sin. The Spirit, Jesus said, would convict of sin, righteousness, and judgment (John 16:8-11). He is the one who delivers a guilty verdict against wrongdoings in our life. He holds our life up to the mirror of God's Word and reveals the inward corruption of our heart. He impresses upon us the urgency of action lest the consequences of sin take their toll.

The Spirit's work reaches his redemptive depth, however, in freeing our life from sin. In Romans 8:13 it is said that by the Spirit we "put to death the misdeeds of the body." This certainly has several aspects to it, not all of which can be touched upon here. I will comment upon one aspect, however, that struck me forcefully several years ago.

As I walked about the Messiah College campus, I noticed that the pin oak trees retained their leaves throughout the winter, in spite of the fact that the frost had killed the leaves in mid-fall, turning them a drab brown. The wind, sleet, snow, and ice of winter caused only a few of these leaves to lose their grip on the branches. When spring arrived, I noticed that the ground was loaded with pin oak leaves. I wondered what finally dislodged them from the branches. I lifted my eyes to the trees in search of an explanation and saw that the buds of spring had caused the old leaves to finally drop off.

Then Romans 8:13 flashed into my mind. Is not this an illustration of the Spirit's power over sin? When one finds redemption in Jesus Christ, sin is put to death in the life. And yet many Christians find some habits difficult to break. There may be besetting sins that defy their best efforts to dislodge them. Sin within seems to withstand their desire to fully follow the Lord. And then a springtime enters their Christian experience. The vital life of the Spirit within causes new buds of the fruit of the Spirit to appear. To their utter amazement, these Christians find the disfiguring leaves of their past expelled from their life. The Spirit, like Christ, sets free from sin.

The Spirit's ministry through believers

Jesus first spoke of the Spirit's strength in terms of his inward ministry to the disciples themselves. But in his last discourses he also spoke of the Spirit's role of strengthening them for witness and service to the world. The disciples would not be alone in their witness about Jesus. The Holy Spirit would be with them as well, giving his testimony of Jesus and thus making the disciples' words effective (John 15:26-27). As the day approached when the disciples would need to be God's messengers to the world, Jesus' words about this ministry of the Spirit became more explicit. Just before his ascension he instructed them to wait in Jerusalem until "clothed with power from on high" (Luke 24:48-49), power from the Holy Spirit to make them witnesses for Jesus throughout the world (Acts 1:8).

Pentecost came as a full demonstration of Jesus' words (Acts 2). The same people who fled for their lives on the night of Jesus' arrest and hid from the authorities for weeks thereafter, suddenly took to the streets and proclaimed Jesus to the very people they had feared so much. They preached Jesus in spite of threats and imprisonment (Acts 3 and 4), persecution and death (Acts 7 and 12), and the opposition of religious and civil authorities. Philip had the courage to preach Jesus to the Samaritans, bitter enemies of the Jews (Acts 8). Peter broke religious tradition and entered a Gentile's home to preach Christ to a Jewish proselyte (Acts 10). And Paul endured long, difficult missionary journeys to introduce both Jews and Gentiles to the Messiah.

Power to witness in the New Testament did not mean the witnesses never experienced fear or failure. In the prayer meeting in Acts 4, the early Christians prayed for courage to witness. They were faced with persecution and needed boldness to continue their witnessing. It took special preparation by the Spirit to get Philip to approach the Ethiopian (Acts 8), Ananias to minister to Paul (Acts 9), and Peter to carry the gospel to the house of a Gentile (Acts 10, 11). Paul admitted to the Corinthians that he began his witness among them "in weakness and fear, and with much trembling" (1 Corinthians 2:1-5; cf. Acts 18:9-11). He asked the Ephesians to pray for him, that he would have the courage to open his mouth to proclaim Christ with boldness during his imprisonment at Rome (Ephesians 6:18-20). The Spirit's clothing the believer with power to witness, then, means a strengthening in spite of normal fears. As tools prove their worth in the using, so the Spirit manifests his power while we engage in witnessing. If we wait for some overpowering experience to banish all fear from our lives, we will not know the Spirit in this way, and little witnessing will get done.

It simply is not true that only outgoing, salesman-type personalities are people filled by the Spirit for witness. While Peter and Paul dominate the accounts in Acts, others proved quite effective, though they were not as outgoing. One thinks of Philip, the deacon who turned evangelist, along with several of his daughters (Acts 21:8-9). There is Dorcas who witnessed by means of her craft as a seamstress (Acts 9:36-42). One could go on and list many who labored with Paul as missionary helpers and appointees, but were considerably more reticient than Paul. My favorite character in Acts is Barnabas. While he took a back seat to Paul, he comforted people wherever he went (and thus earned his surname which meant son of encouragement—Acts 4:36). Barnabas demonstrated the strength of a quiet spirit, yet he was an effective missionary in his own right.

There are a host of Christians, modern Dorcases and Barnabases, who are effectively witnessing for Christ but will never be featured in a book of the world's most recognized witnesses. Stable Christian marriages are a witness to many in a society where more marriages seem to fail than succeed. Those who demonstrate honesty on the job and integrity in business are recognized for their Christian principles. Churches which care for their people and minister to the hurting are getting a message through to neighbors, relatives, and friends more often than they know. This is the Spirit at work in individuals and groups, witnessing by the strength of conviction and compassion.

The life we live and the Christlike things we do are also a preparation for verbal witness. They provide credibility for the verbal message that we share. But we cannot stop short of spoken witness and still succeed in carrying the gospel to the world. This was illustrated for me by a mission executive who told this story during my seminary days.

Traveling on a train on one occasion, he needed a table to do some paper work. The only place he could find access to one was in the dining car, which also served as the liquor bar for the train. Naturally, he had no part with the refreshment others were having, nor their conversation at the bar. After completing his work, he ordered a soft drink and joined with the people in a game of guessing each other's occupations. The group decided he was likely an F.B.I. agent. He had done nothing un-Christian while among them, but until he spoke to them about his job in missions, they had no clear idea he was a Christian. We must do more than let our *life* witness for us. People might well have noticed that we are different, but they will not know *why* we are different until we tell them about Christ.

Many Christians feel guilty about their weakness in spoken witness. How shall they find courage to do it? First, many of our fears stem from not knowing how to do it. Here is where a variety of soul-winning classes have prepared thousands of Christians for personal evangelism. There simply is no substitute, however, for teaming up with an experienced witness and learning how to do it through observation and practice. This is how Jesus trained his disciples and how Paul developed new believers to become effective missionaries. The Spirit works in the Christian fellowship, using those gifted in evangelism to develop the gifts of others for the same ministry.

Secondly, we need to discover here, too, that the Father gives the Holy Spirit to those who ask him (Luke 11:13; cf. Acts 4:23-31). John Zuck is now a pastor near Petersburg, Ontario, Canada. As a young Christian he was troubled about his inability to witness to the men he worked with. When he tried to witness, it seemed his fears accentuated the speech impediment that was part of his life. He felt the responsibility to witness and began to pray that God would strengthen him for it. During meetings in his local church, he prayed for the Spirit to empower his life for witness and believed God had answered his prayer. On the job he found courage to verbalize his faith; even his speech impediment was gone. Now one of his greatest thrills is sharing the gospel with those who need to hear it.

Jesus came to earth to bear witness to the Father. Now his followers have been commissioned with this task. Nothing is more central than this in God's purpose concerning the world. When we come to realize Christ's perspective on people and their need for eternal salvation, we will be in line for God's resources to carry out the task. He will strengthen us through the Spirit to be faithful witnesses.

The Holy Spirit and you

In the closing days of his ministry, Jesus announced the Spirit who would come (John 14 and Acts 1). The second chapter of Acts records the historic coming of the Spirit with such definiteness that to this day Pentecost is a fixed calendar day for Christians, just as Christmas and Easter are. In Peter's message on that first Pentecost, he declared that the Holy Spirit was the Father's promise to every Christian (Acts 2:38-39). Thus the early church showed concern when anyone professed faith in Christ but had not received the Spirit (Acts 8:14-17; 19:1-7). God simply does not want any of his children going through life feeling like orphans. Our bodies are to be the temple of the Holy Spirit (1 Corinthians 6:19), not the empty tenements of an absentee Lord.

The past century has witnessed enormous controversy over the Holy Spirit. To the degree that this discussion has focused people's attention upon the vital role of the Spirit, it has fulfilled an essential role. To the degree that it has distracted people over uncertain questions of "when" and "how" the Spirit comes to an individual, it has been a stumbling block rather than a stepping stone. In these matters the simple, common sense approach is best. The Spirit will come *whenever* our heart is ready for his dwelling, and he will come *however* God sees best to meet our personal needs. The Spirit himself will satisfy the Christian of his presence in the life. He will manifest himself in personal ministries for the believer's welfare and in equipping the disciple for witness concerning Christ. The Father knows how to give good gifts— especially the Holy Spirit—to his people. For our part, the essential thing is that we ask the Father to do it (Luke 11:9-13).

I am the vine; you are the branches. If a man remains in me and I in him, he will bear much fruit; apart from me you can do nothing.

But the fruit of the Spirit is love, joy, peace, patience, kindness, goodness, faithfulness, gentleness and self-control.

John 15:5; Galatians 5:22-23

7

Fruit With God's Label

John 15:1-11; Galatians 5:22-26

If we had the chance to plan and plant the garden of our dreams, many of us would have the time of our life doing it. What couldn't we do if space, finances, and expert resources were unlimited? Maybe we would travel the world to see some of the best gardens, collect ideas on design and available plants, and discover who the people are who could help to construct our dream garden. Many of us would aim for a productive garden. We would include plants, shrubs, and trees that produced foods and other usable products. We would surely aim for a garden that was a thing of beauty—a symmetry of designs and shapes, a kaleidoscope of colors, and a blend of aromas to please the most discriminating nose. Our goal would be to create a garden that would stand as a tribute to our craftsmanship. We would want it to be something with which our name could joyfully be associated.

The "fruit of the Spirit" mentioned particularly in Galatians 5, and intimated elsewhere, is similar to this garden of our dreams. God is the supreme gardener and artist. He desires us to be productive; he wants our character to be Christlike; and he desires us to produce good works. He also wants to make our lives a thing of beauty and balance. His name will be associated with our lives. Thus, he desires us to be a credit to his creative workmanship. Wherever the grace of Jesus Christ triumphs and flourishes, one will find the lives of men and women which stand out as lovely gardens in the midst of otherwise bland and unattractive human landscapes.

Creative life and disciplined labor

Gardening, as in agricultural in general, is the result of both the creative order of God and the domestic efforts of human beings. God has established the natural order of plant life, including its varied methods of reproduction, its conditions of growth, and the produce it develops. The gardener must know these things and plan his activities in accordance with this knowledge. He must prepare the seedbed, cultivate the plants, and harvest them properly. In a fallen world, gardens do not appear naturally; they require a gardener whose efforts insure the desired product.

In the spiritual realm also, this tension between God-given life and human effort is maintained. The holy life results from God's grace, but it is an operation requiring human discipline. Scripture addresses both aspects of the tension and does not try to settle this equation by opting for an either/or stance. Thus, Philippians 2:12-13 says: "Work out your own salvation with fear and trembling, for it is God who works in you to will and to act according to his good purpose." God is at work and we are to work—here grace and discipline are joined in the pursuit of the holy life.

The testimony of 2 Peter 1:3-11 confirms this sense of balance. On the one hand God has granted everything pertaining to the life of godliness, including the promises whereby we actually partake of the divine nature (verses 3 and 4). Yet we must make every effort to add virtue, knowledge, self-control, steadfastness, godliness, brotherly kindness, and love to our faith (verses 5-11). God's grace stands behind our discipline to make it possible, but our discipline must make grace effective in the pursuit of the life pleasing to God.

This chapter on the fruit of the Spirit and the one that follows on disciplines of the holy life probe both sides of this scriptural statement about the holy life. For the sake of specific focus, we do well to note them separately. In doctrine and experience they belong together. If we can hold on to this larger picture, then we can proceed to examine the individual issues.

God's initiative

The first step toward every lovely garden is an ingenious master plan. Before the creation itself, God designed to make man in his own image. The fall of mankind enormously complicated this plan, but it did not negate it. By means of redemption through Jesus Christ (2 Timothy 1:9; 1 Peter 1:1-20), God's ultimate goal remained unchanged. Note Paul's description of it in Ephesians 1:3-4:

> Praise be to the God and Father of our Lord Jesus Christ, who has blessed us in the heavenly realms with every spiritual blessing in Christ. For he chose us in him before the creation of the world to be holy and blameless in his sight.

With bated breath we note that God still intends to make us people in his image—holy as he is holy. He intends to make our lives the garden spot of his grace. He plans for fruitfulness in righteousness that exceeds our most optimistic dreaming.

God's initiative is demonstrated, secondly, in his promises. Immediately following Adam and Eve's sin, God promised a Saviour who would crush the serpent's head (Genesis 3:15). Starting with Abraham and following down into the New Testament, God's covenant terms were filled with divine promises. On one hand, the promises announced the divine plan of redemption. On the other hand, they were the basis of trust in God's faithfulness to meet human needs. The end result was that those who believed God's promises lived differently from those who did not. Faith led to righteousness in those who trusted God.

It works the same today. It is by God's "very great and precious promises" that we are able to "participate in the divine nature and escape the corruption in the world caused by evil desires" (2 Peter 1:4). These are "very great promises" because they announce wonderful divine intentions for our lives. They are "precious" promises because God's resources are adequate to his promises. The term "precious" here is a money word. It means currency that has value equal to its stated amount. Our printed money, for example, has value solely because of the gold and silver reserves which guarantee the stated worth of the paper money. In like manner, God's promises are not inflated; he can deliver the full value of what he has promised. Behind all the fruit of the Spirit stands God's word to make us partakers of his "divine nature." We would not dare to hope for this on our own abilities. Only the guarantee of his word gives us grounds to believe the promise.

God's initiative is revealed, thirdly, in his providence. In spite of the opposition of Satan and the unfaithfulness of Israel, God kept his redemptive covenant with mankind. Historical events and human calendars were subjected to his sovereign will. In the "fulness of time" Christ was born as Savior of the world. His life and ministry carried out God's plan of redemption as promised by the prophets centuries earlier, climaxing in Easter and Pentecost. The Gospels and the book of Acts magnify God's providence in fulfillment of his promise to redeem mankind.

When we look at our spiritual development, we see the same providential hand of God at work. At just the right moment in our life God brought to us the grace needed for our Christian development. As the gardener knows the right time to plant each seed, how and when to fertilize the various plants, how to regulate heat, light, and moisture, and how to overcome pests and diseases, so God knows how to fashion all things so that they work together for good in our lives (Romans 8:28). In every area of spiritual growth, we are dependent upon God's initiative just as plants are upon the gardener's care. We must respond to that care, but apart from it we have no life of our own.

The fruit of the Spirit, then, is based upon God's initiative in the lives of Christians. Rooted in the soil of God's eternal plan to make mankind in the image of their Creator, this fruit springs from the seeds of his redemptive promises. Nourished by his providential direction, our lives experience genuine spiritual growth.

Much fruit

People plant gardens so that they might produce the food products they desire. God also wants our lives to be productive. Jesus' parable of the vine in John 15 underscores this point. The branch that bears "no fruit" is taken away and destroyed by fire. Branches that bear fruit are pruned so they might bear "more fruit." It is by bearing "much fruit" that the Father is glorified and people demonstrate that they are disciples of Jesus. Productivity is clearly God's design with respect to his people.

In Jesus' parable of the vine, he illustrates an inseparable relationship between the quality of the branches and the quantity of the fruit. Thus, he speaks about the necessity of pruning if the vine is to produce much fruit. In Galatians 5 Paul has a similar concern. He talks about "crucifying the sinful nature" if the fruit of the Spirit is to illumine our good works. Perhaps some human interest stories can help us grasp what these Scriptures emphasize.

Frank Laubach possibly did more to reduce illiteracy around the world through his "each one teach one" campaign than any other person of this century. But the early days of his missionary work in the Philippines carried no hint that he would ever be so useful. His ministry bore little fruit, and he had antagonized many of the Moslem people he wished to convert by his combative stance against them. On the mountainside above the village where he was serving, brooding over his failure, he was convicted by the Spirit of God that he should ask forgiveness of the Moslem teachers for his actions toward them. He obeyed the Lord in true contriteness of heart. The teachers were most surprised by this change in his manner, but it made a difference in his relationship with them.

God had begun to make a new person of Frank Laubach. Now his witness began to be effective. Eventually he became an ambassador for Christ around the world. In his advanced years, he visited Asbury Seminary campus for extended periods of time. In meeting the man, one was impressed with his love, his humility, and his spirit of servanthood. One then understood the secret of his great usefulness. God had pruned away the things in his life which hindered the bearing of fruit for the kingdom. A transformed character was the key to his extensive good works.

Ian Maclaren tells the story of a Scottish youth about to preach his first sermon in his first pastoral assignment. He spent all week on it, hoping to justify his training and his reputation as a young scholar. On Saturday he discussed his sermon with his maiden aunt, who had moved into the manse to be his housekeeper. She reminded him that the parishioners were simple folk who needed a word from God to face the realities of life. She reminded him of his dying mother's words, five years earlier, when she told him that if God ever called him to preach, he was to make it his goal to "speak a good word for Jesus." His aunt then retired to her room to pray for him, while he went to his room to rehearse his sermon for the next day.

The young preacher's soul was in turmoil. He realized that too much of his motivation for preaching was a desire to glorify his talents rather than to glorify Christ. The memory of his mother's words exerted a gracious influence over his heart. Finally he surrendered his masterpiece to the flames in the fireplace. In a renewed effort of preparation he sought to frame a "good word for Jesus." When he stepped into the pulpit the next day, he spoke with a humble spirit and an overflowing heart. The presence of God rested upon the service, and the congregation accepted their youthful pastor with affection. In his Saturday vigil he had "crucified the flesh" with its passions and desires. When Sunday dawned—the Lord's day, the day of resurrection—the fruit of the Spirit issued forth in splendor.[1]

Christian usefulness ("much fruit") is not simply a matter of statistics. It is not measured by dollars given, by years served, or by the number of people to which one ministers. It is measured by faithfulness to the task one is given, by stewardship of the gifts and resources God has given, and by the love of God and men which motivates our service. This is the kind of fruit Jesus said would last (John 15:16). It was the kind of fruit that characterized his ministry, and, if we abide in the vine, it is the produce he will develop in us as well.

---

[1]Ian Maclaren, *Beside the Bonnie Brier Bush.* New York: Dodd, Mead and Company, 1895, pp. 85-100.

The good and the beautiful

One characteristic of a good garden is productivity; another is its aesthetic impression—the impression of beauty it conveys to the beholder. Here one thinks of the symmetry of shapes and designs, the balance of colors, and the variety of impressions. God has given us the capacity to enjoy beauty, and when we behold the natural world, beauty seems to be one of the attributes of God's own nature. This sense of beauty and proportion is not confined solely to the natural realm; there is a sense in which it permeates the spiritual domain as well.

What was it that made Jesus so attractive in his earthly ministry and still appeals to those who meet him in Scripture? One's immediate impression is to cite his absolute goodness—he was holiness personified. But that does not fully grasp his appeal. We have all known people whose lives were above reproach, many whom we would call holy and good, yet we did not find them to be attractive personalities. Somehow their goodness seemed like a distortion of life; it was goodness that in some way lacked proportion. Jesus was different! There was never a more balanced personality; all his qualities seemed to be in perfect proportion. His was a natural goodness—it seemed to fit his total life, holding all of it in perfect harmony. With Jesus the good was made beautiful, and we find that kind of goodness most appealing.

The fruit of the Spirit (Galatians 5:22-23) likewise is appealing. Most people would admit that this passage describes the type person they would like to be. Even though the brief list of nine qualities is suggestive rather than exhaustive, there is the sense of balance, proportion, and attractiveness in the whole. These qualities address the composite nature of human personality and the full range of human relationships.

It is so easy for us to become one-dimensional Christians, exaggerating one quality and neglecting others. But God wants us to be well-balanced. Note, for example, the successive listing of kindness *(chrēstotēs)* and goodness *(agathōsune).* Goodness sees truth according to clearly defined standards of right and wrong. It implies a zealousness for the right that could lead to aggressive stances on behalf of principles. Kindness, however, denotes wholesomeness and graciousness. It seeks that which is profitable for people, avoiding abruptness and severity. Here then, are complementary virtues essential to our interaction with others. Emphasized in isolation, they would distort human relationships. Taken together, they enable us to "speak the truth with love" (See Ephesians 4:15). Kindness clothes goodness with humility, patience, and gentleness, and thus makes it attractive and winsome.

The Book of Revelation speaks of the "tree of life" with its twelve kinds of fruit, one for each month of the year (Revelation 22:2). Well-planned gardens are like this—they are a mixture of varieties, so something is always at the fruit-bearing stage. So, too, is the fruit of the Spirit in its several varieties. Different occasions in life require varied responses. For the Christian life to be lovely, it needs the complete assortment of the fruit of the Spirit, fruit for every season of the life.

The writer to the Hebrews believed God could so equip Christians that their lives would be a thing of beauty. Thus, he prayed:

> May the God of peace, who through the blood of the eternal covenant brought back from the dead our Lord Jesus, that great Shepherd of the sheep, equip you with everything good for doing his will, and may he work in us what is pleasing to him, through Jesus Christ, to whom be glory for ever and ever. Amen. (Hebrews 13:20-21)

Note the stress upon the complete equipping to do God's good will. Note also that the result is a life "pleasing to him" (RSV). This last expression is an artistic one in the original language. It suggests that God can so develop the garden of our life that it becomes a work of art which brings pleasure to the Creator-Artist.

The image of God as artist fits well with the creation story of Genesis 1 and 2. Here God also planted a garden and called it Eden. He viewed each thing he had made and pronounced it good. But only after he created Adam and Eve could he view the whole and pronounce it very good. We generally think of God's artistic genius in relation to the beauties of the natural creation. But it is really people that are God's greatest work of art. Sin has distorted this picture so that we frequently do not see beauty in human lives. Yet through the fruit of the Spirit, God is involved in the greatest art reclamation program of history, restoring that beauty of the divine image so disastrously damaged by the fall. He is working to fashion gardens out of human wastelands, so as to restore creation to its original paradise.

The name on the fruit

When the Christmas season of 1983 brought freezing weather to the citrus area of southern United States, the fruit producers acted to restrict shipments of fruit until their quality was guaranteed. They did not want something bearing their label to ruin their reputation of producing quality fruit. As Christians we bear the stamp of God's name upon our lives. God is also concerned about the character of his name. That is why he labors to produce quality fruit in us. Our submission to his workmanship will result in glory to his name and the advertisement of his grace to those who need it. To wear God's trademark, we must be subject to his quality control program.

For this very reason, make every effort to add to your faith goodness; and to goodness, knowledge; and to knowledge, self-control; and to self-control, perseverance; and to perseverance, godliness; and to godliness, brotherly kindness; and to brotherly kindness, love.

2 Peter 1:5-7

8

Discipline: A Good Christian Word

Mark 8:34-38; 2 Peter 1:1-11

Early Sunday morning, January 24, 1965, a Sunday school teacher in Tallahassee, Florida, was reviewing his lesson for the day. His local congregation, the John Wesley Methodist Church, seemed to need some inspiration for its people to be motivated for God. It sounds like the all-too-familiar church story. There were apparent needs: attendance at services should have been better, there was a shortage of Sunday school teachers, the choir was very small, and the budget was not being met.

He had recently begun a series of lessons with the Christian Home-Builders Class (ages 21-35) which was designed to help them formulate a Christian life that really mattered. Discouraged that the class members did not seem to have a sense of direction for spiritual growth, he turned to God in prayer for the necessary wisdom to motivate them. In the next twenty minutes, the Lord inspired him to write down a brief program for spiritual discipline. Called "The Ten Brave Christians" program, it gave simple directions for five basic Christian disciplines: (1) weekly gathering for group prayer, (2) giving two hours of one's time weekly for use in some phase of the church's life and ministry, (3) tithing (1/10 of the income), (4) daily personal devotions (5:30-6:00 a.m.), and (5) witnessing to others about God's working in one's life.

He shared this program with the Sunday school class,

asking those who were willing to give these disciplines a one month trial to sign a commitment card and send it to him in the mail. Twenty-two people agreed to try the discipline experiment during the month of March. The last Sunday of the month, five participants shared with the congregation what God had done in their lives that month. It sparked a spiritual renewal in the congregation, the results of which were increased attendance at services, an over-subscribed budget (plus a significant financial project to expand church facilities), enough Sunday school teacher volunteers for a ratio of one teacher for every eight students, and—most of all—numerous individuals whose lives began to matter to them, their community, and their God.[1]

Spiritual disciplines do make a vast difference in the quality of the Christian life. The scriptural idea for discipline is a system of training. It serves the Christian like a training program prepares the athlete. Many Christians need to learn the practical methods of spiritual discipline that put them in shape to perform well in their Christian life.

The discipline of Bible study

From the beginning of God's dealings with mankind, God has made himself known to man through his communicated word. The inspired word is a primary discipline of the people of God. It shapes our thoughts, fashions our affections, motivates our wills, and influences the totality

---

[1]For more information see the twenty-seven page booklet written by Sam E. Teague; *The John Wesley—Great Experiment: Wanted Ten Brave Christians*. Atlanta: Spiritual Life Publishers, 1965. Booklets can be obtained by writing to Brave Christian Associates, P.O. Box 987, Tallahassee, Florida 32301

ships. There is virtually no growth in the
vhich is not tied directly to the discipline of
th its private and public readings.

mothy 3:16-17 puts the discipline of Scrip-
ul a framework as any passage of the Bible:
ure is God-breathed and is useful for
rebuking, correcting and training in
ness, so that the man of God may be
ly equipped for every good work.

function of Scripture is to give instruction
ebuke (convict of) wrong and to restore to
to train (discipline, cf. Ephesians 6:4 where
d is used) the Christian in righteousness.
o completely equip the Christian for every
here is an emphasis here upon balance and
he total Scripture, for the total person, for a
ion in godly living. Each of us readily identi-
rite passages of Scripture, but we need to
tudy of the Bible in its entirety, hearing what
y to us from every part of it. This will take
uires our following some type of plan for
tudy that enables us to be acquainted with
le. What is important is that we get started
ure begin to minister to our total needs.

sonal study of the Bible is only part of the
ne Word. In order to be fully equipped, we
discipline of group learning in the Scripture.
e Colossians (3:16), Paul said, "Let the word
ell in you richly as you teach and admonish
with all wisdom, and as you sing psalms,
iritual songs with gratitude in your hearts to
y group God has gifted some to teach and
ord. The church has recognized these per-
rged them with the responsibility to preach

the "whole counsel of God" (Acts 20:27). God's Word
also learned from the shared insights of believers as th
engage in Bible study together. No one understands ev
facet of truth contained in the Bible. Our understandi
can only be enriched as we share with one another. He
too, is a corrective factor against personal errors in t
interpretation and the application of Scripture.

Second Corinthians 3:1-4:6 highlights the effect
God's Word in transforming our life. Due to the minist
of the Spirit illuminating the Scripture and imprinting
upon our lives, the Scripture is not some dull written co
but it is life and freedom in their highest sense. Moses' fa
absorbed the glory of the Lord on Mt. Sinai while G
gave him the law. When he came down from the mou
tain, his face shone with the light of God's glory. So, P
says, we encounter the glory of God in his Word, and
transforms us into the very image of our Lord, from o
degree of glory to another. Mark it down—wherever y
find a Christlike person, you will find a person deep
involved with the Word of God!

The discipline of prayer

Prayer, in and of itself, is a powerful discipline, but
probably reaches its greatest strength when combin
with the discipline of the Scripture. Prayer acknowledg
our need of help to understand the Scripture that we re
The Psalmist prayed, "Open my eyes that I may see wo
derful things in your law" (119:18). In the same spirit, Jo
Wesley revealed what he did when he did not immediat
understand a part of the Bible.

> In his presence I open, I read his book; for this
> end, to find the way to heaven. Is there a doubt
> concerning the meaning of what I read? Does
> anything appear dark or intricate? I lift up my
> eyes to the Father of lights:—"Lord, is it not thy

word, 'If any man lack wisdom, let him ask of God?' Thou 'givest liberally, and upbraidest not.' Thou has said, 'If any be willing to do thy will, he shall know.' I am willing to do, let me know, thy will." I then search after and consider parallel passages of Scripture, "comparing spiritual things with spiritual." I meditate thereon with all the attention and earnestness of which my mind is capable. If any doubt still remains, I consult those who are experienced in the things of God; and then the writings whereby being dead, they yet speak. And what I thus learn, that I teach.[2]

Jesus promised the teaching ministry of the Holy Spirit to his disciples, so they would be led into all truth according to what Jesus taught while on earth (John 14:26). Prayer in the course of the study of Scripture acknowledges this personal teaching ministry of the Spirit.

The study of Scripture, in turn, gives a natural focus to our praying. If the word instructs, prayer tries to fasten upon the lesson to be grasped. If the Bible convicts of sin, prayer turns into confession and the earnest petition that God would cleanse the heart and purify one's life. Where the Scripture shows that one is not properly aligned with God's will, prayer becomes a statement of submission to God. Prayer becomes a plea for strength and perseverance in those areas of crossbearing and service which the New Testament enjoins as the way of Jesus. The message of the Bible, then, reveals those things God would have us to pray about.

Prayer is a vast discipline, covering a wide range of forms, techniques, and areas of interest. If we want to improve our praying, we should note the examples of

---

[2]John Wesley, *Works*, V, pp. 3-4.

prayer in the Bible. We should consider how the godly prayed and for what they prayed. No one prayer ever fits every situation, but the Lord's Prayer (Matthew 6:9-13) serves as a model prayer in the things it suggests. It focuses upon different issues that need to be combined in a good prayer life.

First, prayer is seen as an intimate conversation with God. We come to one who wills to be known as Father. This says we pray knowing that we are loved and cared for. We do not need to force concessions out of a reluctant deity. Rather, the Father wants to give good things to his children. Still, there is a reverence that must guard the most intimate relationships of life. God's name is hallowed, reverenced in a class by itself, meriting our singular devotion. Thus worship, adoration, praise, and thanksgiving must become as much a matter of our praying as the voicing of our needs. God is the high and holy one who inhabits eternity; he also dwells with those of contrite heart (Isaiah 57:15). Learning to keep this balance in prayer—reverence and intimacy—will bring the proper attitude to our praying.

Second, the Lord's prayer points to a balance between our petitions regarding "daily bread" and the concerns of the kingdom. It is consistent with the understanding of God as our Father to know that any concern of life which disturbs our peace is a legitimate matter for prayer. We are told to come boldly with our requests (Hebrews 4:16), knowing that God will not scold us about pestering him with our personal needs (James 1:5). Yet so often our praying rises no higher than this. In the rest of Matthew 6, Jesus taught us that even our legitimate needs of life must be put into the context of the kingdom and what God wills for the world. There are many issues of greater importance than food and shelter, and there are vast needs in the world beyond our own concerns.

There are some very practical helps for our prayer discipline in this regard. Praying with others—prayer partners, family worship, small groups, congregational prayer,—helps us to see the larger work of God. When we move to the issues on which two or three can agree on earth concerning the will of God, we have already broken through the selfish confines of our own needs. Many have found the keeping of a prayer list does the same thing. My personal devotional folder contains the latest prayer letters of several church agencies and personal friends, in addition to lists of people I feel I should pray for. I find this a necessary discipline for myself. It not only keeps my mind from straying while in prayer, but it also assures that prayer times focus on the needs of the kingdom and not just my urgent needs of the moment.

The last petitions of the Lord's Prayer call attention to a third cluster of concerns. Coupled with our petitions for forgiveness are two complementary ones: forgiveness of those who have wronged us, and an eagerness to be so led of the Lord as to be delivered from evil in the hour of temptation. Here we see prayer as schooling in godliness, learning to extend forgiveness as well as receive it, and learning to take on God's attitude toward sin in resisting evil.

There is a vital connection between prayer and spiritual maturity. The mature disciples give greater attention to the worship of God, to the kingdom and God's will respecting it, and to extending forgiveness to others as well as avoiding evil. It is also true that the effort to go beyond mere personal needs in our praying—to focus upon our Lord, the work of his kingdom, and the character of the saint—is the very pathway to spiritual growth and maturation.

The discipline of fellowship

Part of the process of writing this book was to invite readers of the *Evangelical Visitor* to share their own story regarding topics covered in the book. Edwin Kessler, of Reynoldsville, Pennsylvania, shared his thoughts and experiences regarding the place of fellowship in his Christian experience.

> The brotherhood of believers, our adoption into the family of God, has always had particular emphasis in the Brethren in Christ Church. This means that our home is in the kingdom of God, and, as such, we can be described as aliens here on earth. Thus, the Christian fellowship which the church provides is a reflection of the Good Shepherd tending his flock in strange pastures. Our fellowship with one another builds a home away from home.

Edwin went on to describe how the fellowship of the Free Grace congregation at Millersburg, Pennsylvania, strongly influenced him at crucial points of his life. He was not a believer when he first attended services there. The quality of fellowship he sensed among them, however, was a principal factor in drawing him to Christ. At the crucial stage of a young believer, fellowship determined his spiritual growth through "warm greetings (smiles with every loving handshake), reassuring prayers, challenging sermons, illuminating lessons, and a leadership to follow." One of the strong benefits of this association was marriage to a supportive Christian woman in the congregation, thus carrying Christian fellowship into the practical details of life in the home. Most recently he has relied on the counsel of the group in determining a call to the ministry and for guidance in securing the needed training. He is aware that his brothers and sisters in the Lord are not perfect, but this seems insignificant when viewed against the positive benefits such fellowship has meant to him as a Christian.

Mr. Kessler's account touches upon many of the positive benefits of fellowship. Fellowship connotes all the warmth of family life. Just as our families help us cope with life and relationships outside the home, so the church provides the disciple with support for relationships in the world. Here we are cared for and learn to care. It is the life of the body which nurtures our growth, monitors our progress, and restores us when we falter and fall. The strong help the weak, and the self-motivators inspire the followers to become active in some phase of Christian activity.

We are social beings, made for group life. Our values, thoughts, and actions are largely shaped by the significant people around us. The fellowship of believers becomes our greatest weapon against the pressure of the world to make us conform to its secular culture. It also brings joy to discipleship by making it a shared pilgrimage. Devotional life, worship, stewardship, witness, and service all take on new luster when we can engage in them with others. The stronger our ties become to the family of God, the more healthy our own sense of Christian personhood becomes.

Fellowship fosters a sense of accountability. Our vows of membership, linking us to one another, publicly commit us to certain obligations. We submit to the instruction and the correction of the group, following the guidelines of our Lord in Matthew 18:15-22. This establishes a pattern for those times in which we may need to be the confessors (James 5:16), seeking restoration with the help of the group. It also projects the spirit of love with which we may need to confront an erring Christian (Galatians 6:1-5) and offer to him or her the peace of Christ's reconciliation (John 20:22-23).

The discipline of stewardship

In the parables on the talents (Matthew 25:14-30) and the minas (Luke 19:11-27; pounds in KJV and RSV), there is the recognition that personal resources differ. However, the point is made that faithfulness will increase the productivity of the resources that we have. It is so easy to envy those who seem to have greater assets in a given area than we do, and completely overlook their careful stewardship which resulted in the growth of their resources. Investing our resources is a key factor in growth in the holy life.

How often have you said, "If I had more time, I . . ."? Yet every day has twenty-four hours and every week has seven days. Some people get more done because they manage their time better. They have decided what is really important in life and invest their time in those concerns. Howard F. Landis, Sr., an octogenarian from Souderton, Pennsylvania, wrote of the discipline of time in his life.

> The Lord does not seem to be pleased with me being too much interested in things of an entertaining nature. The Holy Spirit seems to want all my time that's possible. I have never owned a TV set. I don't condemn people that have one. I have watched TV already, but I feel that the Lord could be better served by me without one. The Holy Spirit tells me it would take too much of his time.

For years Brother Landis has followed a particular calling to write letters of encouragement to fellow Christians, particularly ministers and missionaries. I have personally been blessed by this ministry of his, and wonder how many others have been touched by this saint who has been disciplining the resource of time in his life for nearly fifty years. Think of the difference an hour or two a day makes for the kingdom when fifty years are added up.

That is not to say that God wants his people to be compulsive workaholics. Some of us need to be reminded that our business is really in service to God rather than a service to our personal ego. About a year ago I was reviewing with the Lord in my prayer time my schedule of church responsibilities, feeling my need to get all of them accomplished. I was not anticipating the quiet response of the Spirit, for God put this thought into my mind: "If you are too busy, then some things you are doing are not my will for you, because I do not overwork my servants." Some of the things we describe as spiritual problems in our lives are really physical or emotional at root. Treating our bodies and minds with greater care would make life more enjoyable and project a better witness for Christ than our busy lives often do.

Some of us are discovering that we have accumulated material things faster than we have developed a good sense of stewardship regarding them. These material possessions have become obstacles in our path in the marathon of life. We need some plan whereby we can begin to deal responsibly with our material resources. The biblical tithe (ten percent of one's income) is an introductory level discipline in this respect. It gives us a system to follow which is reinforced by the weekly offerings practiced by the congregation. It should not stop there, however. Some need to take the discipline of giving to the second tithe, or the third tithe. We can approach stewardship in other areas as well: less income, more simple lifestyle, sharing our things with a larger group of users, etc. Material discipline aims to correct our self-centered use of the created world in order to more fully serve the needs of others. It attempts to realize the words of the Lord that "it is more blessed to give than to receive" (Acts 20:35).

Far too many of us are like the man in Jesus' parable, who buried the treasure his Lord gave him. If we could have a God's-eye view of any given congregation gathered for worship, it would make us weep. Like some vast human junkyard, talents are scattered about, deteriorating through lack of use. Some depreciate their gifts out of a false sense of humility, unwilling to use them for God lest they fail in the effort. Others see their abilities in only one dimension. They have never thought that the same talent which makes them successful in the world of employment could have an application in the affairs of the home, the community, or the church. Some neglect the additional training which could develop their abilities for greater usefulness. If we would grow spiritually, then we must acknowledge the particular gifts God has given us and engage them for good use.

The reward of discipline

Spiritual disciplines are not a program for inflicting punishment upon ourselves. They are the means for channeling our inner energy to accomplish creative things. Initially they may require concentrated effort, but then the rewards for our effort start to pay out handsome dividends. Like a jogger who first begins to run under doctor's orders, but then looks forward to doing his daily run because it feels so good, spiritual disciplines make one enjoy his or her Christian walk. As the people in John Wesley Methodist Church discovered, discipline opens the door to the blessings of God.

After this the Lord appointed seventy-two others and sent them two by two ahead of him to every town and place where he was about to go. He told them, "The harvest is plentiful, but the workers are few. Ask the Lord of the harvest, therefore, to send out workers into his harvest field."

Luke 10:1-2

9

Gifted For Service

Luke 10:1-11, 17-20; 1 Corinthians 12:4-11, 14-26

"Service" is one of those words which falls too easily from the lips of Christians. Often it is a general term for doing things for others. But Jesus plainly told us that much of our doing good to others fails to achieve the level of Christian service (Matthew 5:43-48). Often it has become nothing more than social convention—doing nice things for those who will, in turn, do nice things for us. Christian service involves doing good for those who cannot return it, loving and serving even when it is not convenient, and helping those whose ways do not readily endear them to us.

Christian service requires equipping by the Spirit of God. The early disciples of Jesus were eager to share the news of his resurrection. But Jesus refused to turn them loose on the world merely on the strength of their enthusiasm. He commanded them to stay in Jerusalem until empowered by the Spirit from on high. When we enter into Christ's ministry to the world, we begin to feel the weight of the cross—all the needs and the hurts of a vast world of people. We face the opposition of Satan in the multiplied factors that work against Christian truth and love. Unless strengthened and gifted by the Holy Spirit, we cannot serve nor survive in the depressing world of human need.

Christ's love and Christ's power—these must come together in the believer's life if Christian service is to be a reality.

Jesus' model of service

When Jesus came to his hometown of Nazareth to preach his first sermon to his neighbors (Luke 4:16-30), he chose the opening verses of Isaiah 61 for his text:

The Spirit of the Sovereign Lord is on me,
   because the Lord has anointed me
   to preach good news to the poor.
He has sent me to bind up the broken hearted,
   to proclaim freedom for the captives
   and release for the prisoners,
   to proclaim the year of the Lord's favor . . .

(Isaiah 61:1-2).

These words highlight the comprehensive nature of Jesus' ministry—salvation of souls and bodies, minds and relationships. For these multiplied tasks he was anointed by the Spirit at his baptism, initiating his work as the Messiah.

During the days of his ministry, Jesus had no home to call his own. Traveling most of the time, he had to eat and sleep according to the accommodations at hand. Always there seemed to be people about him, claiming his attention and begging his help. In order to be alone, he had to pray while others slept. When he did seek quiet retreat with his disciples, it was only a temporary measure for renewal of vital energies. Then he plunged back into ministering to human need. His was a life of service, a demonstration that the holy life is a life lived on behalf of others.

The servant theme was at the heart of his training of his disciples. He emphasized it in his teaching, and he was the living model of servanthood before them. He called seventy of his disciples to himself one day and empowered them to go out and practice servanthood in preaching the gospel, healing diseases, and casting out demons. As his ministry drew to a close, he spoke more pointedly of the disciples' role as servants of the kingdom. In the parable of the sheep and the goats (Matthew 25:31-46), Jesus emphasized that feeding the hungry, clothing the naked, and visiting the sick and those in prison was the standard by which his people would be judged. Fearing that the disciples still had not caught the point, he washed their feet, relating this act to the servanthood role he expected of them (John 13:1-17).

It is clear, then, that any concept of the holy life is un-Christian if it stops short of active witness and service on behalf of God's kingdom. Jesus lived and died on behalf of others' needs. When he asks us to take up his cross and follow him, he is asking us to live in this spirit of servanthood.

Anointing for service

The motivation for service is love; the power for service is the anointing of the Holy Spirit. These are complementary truths; both are required for service. This is of such importance that we need to understand these matters well.

When one asks *why* God redeemed the world, the answer is love (John 3:16). This was also the motive behind every healing, every miracle, and every compassionate deed Jesus performed. He loved and thus he ministered.

But when we ask *how* Jesus did these things, the answer is by the anointing of the Holy Spirit which equipped him for this ministry on earth. Though he was the Son of God, yet he needed the anointing of the Spirit to inaugurate his ministry to human need. Jesus' quotation from Isaiah 61 emphasized this fact: "The Spirit of the

Lord is on me, because he has anointed me to preach good news . . ." (Luke 4:18). The early church understood this—note Peter's message in the house of Cornelius: "God anointed Jesus of Nazareth with the Holy Spirit and power, . . . he went around doing good and healing all who were under the power of the devil, because God was with him" (Acts 10:38).

Here, too, the servant must be like his Lord. It is one thing to be "compelled by the love of Christ" (2 Corinthians 5:14) and have compassion for people in need. It is quite another thing to be able to minister to that need. Like the disciples who were unable to heal the child brought to them (Mark 9:14-29), Christians can be confronted by needs that move them to compassion, but which they are incapable of relieving. That is, they are unable unless anointed by the Holy Spirit as was their Lord! Before Jesus sent out the seventy disciples to do his work, he gave them power to heal and to cast out demons. So, too, before he left his disciples to return to the Father, Jesus charged them not to leave Jerusalem until they were endued with the Spirit and his power. The book of Acts subsequently records the apostles' ministry of preaching the gospel, healing the sick, and casting out demons, which was accomplished in the power of the Holy Spirit. Christ not only asked his followers to serve as he served, he also provided that the same equipping Spirit would empower us for the task which had anointed him for ministry.

The imperative need for the church in every age is to know the anointing of the Spirit upon its ministry. Otherwise the church's ministry fails to be as comprehensive or as effective as it might be. Sin is as rampant, Satan is as active, and human need is as evident as it was in the first century of the Christian era. But "Jesus Christ is the same yesterday and today and forever" (Hebrews 13:8). He desires the Christian ministry to the world to be as effective now as it was for his earliest followers. The Holy Spirit is the key to twentieth century service just as he was in the first century.

The gifts of the Spirit

There are four passages in the New Testament where the gifts of the Spirit are listed to some extent. They are: (1) Romans 12:6-8; (2) 1 Corinthians 12:8-10, and 28-30; (3) Ephesians 4:11; and (4) 1 Peter 4:10-11. Several general comments may be in order before looking more particularly at the types of gifts that are mentioned. First, there is no indication that the list of gifts is exhaustive. At no two places is the list exactly the same. Therefore, those that are listed are likely suggestive rather than a comprehensive naming of all the possible gifts. The fact that one's abilities do not seem to be named in any of the lists is no indication that one is not gifted by the Spirit.

Second, the lists include different aspects of spiritual gifts. Included are abilities, functions, and offices. Thus, for example, one's *abilities* might include the word of wisdom and word of knowledge. These would *function* well in the role of teaching. Teaching could be part of the *office* of an apostle or of a pastor-teacher. Thus the same spiritual gift could go under different titles depending upon the perspective from which it is viewed.

Third, the gifts of the Spirit seem to include both natural talent and special, supernaturally-given abilities. For example, the natural abilities that made Paul a leading Jewish rabbi were put to the service of Jesus Christ at his conversion. God then utilized these natural abilities in making Paul the premier missionary of the first century. But only after his conversion did Paul receive the ability to minister healing and the authority of the apostolic office. These were supernaturally bestowed for his task of planting and administering the church in Gentile lands. Thus, whether by an act of dedication we surrender our natural abilities to the Spirit's control, or we are endowed with a special gift(s) by a personal experience of the Spirit in our lives, the key factor is the anointing of the Holy Spirit.

A fourth fact is that the gifts of the Spirit are developed in the context of the church as the body of Christ. No one person has all the gifts of the Spirit, and every Christian has some gift(s). It is the task of the church to help Christians discover and develop their particular gifts. It should encourage people to exercise their gifts according to principles laid down in Scripture regarding their proper use (1 Corinthians 13 and 14). The gifts are not ends in themselves; they must be evaluated according to their impact upon the community of faith and the tasks the Lord has committed to it.

The ministries of the spiritual gifts

Since there are so many different types of spiritual gifts, it might be helpful to understand their usefulness in terms of several general areas of ministry. First, many gifts help the church to minister to its own need. Second, another group of gifts equip the church to witness to the world. A third category could be called service gifts since they enable Christians to give aid of a more material nature.

Gifts for the church

Ephesians 4:11-16 is the classic expression of the use of the gifts for the spiritual growth of the church.

It was he who gave some to be apostles, some to be prophets, some to be evangelists, and some to be pastors and teachers, to prepare God's people for works of service, so that the body of Christ may be built up until we all reach unity in the faith and knowledge of the Son of God and

become mature, attaining to the whole measure
of the fullness of Christ.

Then we will no longer be infants, tossed back
and forth by the waves, and blown here and
there by every wind of teaching and by the
cunning and craftiness of men in their deceitful
scheming. Instead, speaking the truth in love, we
will in all things grow up into him who is the
Head, that is Christ. From him the whole body,
joined and held together by every supporting
ligament, grows and builds itself up in love, as
each part does its work.

At first glance this seems to focus the gifts in upon the
church instead of outward to the needs of the world. It
almost looks like one more example of the church living
only for itself. And that is a very real danger in the use of
spiritual gifts, but it is not what God intends.

The gifts must minister to believers because Christians are people with needs like any other human being.
Their bodies get sick, their loved ones die, they suffer from
natural disasters, and they are persecuted for their beliefs.
Spiritually they need to be taught the Word, they need
help in combatting Satan, and they need answers to their
prayers. Thus, Christians stand in need of gifted spiritual
leadership, stimulation of their faith, the comfort of those
who minister to their personal needs, and miracles of
grace on their behalf.

Moreover, would you trust a farmer to feed you who
could not produce enough for his own family? Would you
hire a carpenter if the house he built for himself collapsed?
Could you place confidence in a physician who was always
ill? In like manner the church must first minister to its
own needs, or no one will trust its witness or welcome its
service. As things sometimes stand, one of the greatest

obstacles for the church in service is its own disordered house.

It is not at all surprising, then, that so many of the gifts of the Spirit are aimed at some service to the church itself. It is the church which is reaching for maturity and completeness in its own body life that has the potential to become a servant to the world. As long as it can view edification as necessary for servanthood, and does not let ministering to itself become its sole object, the church is following the divine plan for the use of the gifts.

In reality, edification and servanthood are constantly going on as complementary ministries of the gifts of the Spirit. No church ever arrives at perfection, if for no other reason than the fact that its members are at all different stages of growth. So if we wait until all the imperfections are removed from the church, we will never begin a ministry in the world. Thus, some of the energies of the spiritual gifts are focused upon the development of the body, while at the same time other believers through their gifts are ministering to the world. There is a natural rhythm to the Christian life of gathering for fellowship and dispersing for service. Logically, edification is a prerequisite to service, but it does not always precede it in time sequences. In fact, some of our greatest needs for edification follow intensive times of ministry to others.

Gifts for witness

Jesus' last great concern for his disciples was that they would be endued (or clothed) with the Spirit for witness (Luke 24:48-49; Acts 1:8). The immediate result of Pentecost was that they began their witness to the people of Jerusalem. Subsequent chapters trace the expansion of this missionary task to surrounding areas and peoples, until the gospel of Christ had reached Rome, the capital of the empire.

The application of Joel's prophecy to the miracle of Pentecost clearly points out that the Spirit's ministry is to make every Christian a witness for Christ (Acts 2:17-18, 39). The gift of prophecy mentioned here (as also in 1 Corinthians 14) means being spokespersons for God rather than predictors of the future. So we are not amiss to label this gift as the gift of witness, a gift intended for every believer. In the early church, as in every subsequent age of the church, there were individuals who seemed to possess this gift in a unique measure. Among these were the apostles, evangelists, prophets, and teachers who were the earliest missionaries of the church. The New Testament is largely a missionary document; and the church in any age which seeks to be obedient to the Spirit will be committed emphatically to evangelism and missions.

In Acts 2 the gift of speaking in tongues was a witness gift. Not only did it attract the attention of the crowd, it also became the means of sharing God's good news with people from at least fifteen different language groups. One notes with interest the cross-cultural contexts of three other settings in Acts where tongues were involved with the reception of the Spirit: Samaria (Acts 8), the house of Cornelius (Acts 10), and at Ephesus (Acts 19).

Why was this gift manifested in these settings, since the people already could communicate to each other in a common language? Perhaps the key is given in Acts 2:8: "Each of us hears them in his own native language." Language is the cultural code of a given people; it is the key to the way they think. God sought a means of witness that made the gospel personal to every culture, given in thought patterns native to them. And it is still true today that any effective program of evangelism must come through the cultural medium of the people. One hears of rare cases where witness is made possible through an outburst of speech in tongues not learned by the witnesses. More often, as Christians attempt to share the good news across language and cultural barriers, God has providentially led to a linguistic bridge, which makes the gospel understandable to a people for whom its concepts were previously unintelligible. The book *Peace Child* by Donald Richardson is one recent example of this type.

We should note that healings became evangelistic tools as well. A few examples from Acts will illustrate the point. The healing of the lame man outside the Temple (Acts 3) led to a dramatic increase in the number of converts (Acts 4:4). Healing a bed-ridden man at Lydda helped the citizens of that region to turn to the Lord (Acts 9). The healing of a lame man at Lystra was instrumental in planting the church in that city (Acts 14). And Paul's ministry to Asia from Ephesus was enhanced by miracles of healing (Acts 19).

Other miracles had the same function. One thinks quickly of the miraculous escape of Peter and John from prison (Acts 5), the raising of Dorcas from the dead (Acts 9), the prison earthquake at Philippi (Acts 16), and Paul's preservation in spite of shipwreck (Acts 27-28). Miracles affecting those possessed by evil spirits also assisted in the spread of the gospel (Acts 13:6-12; 16:16-18).

Healings, miracles, and casting out of demons—these were part of Jesus' witness in Palestine and part of the ministry of the seventy he sent out. The early Christians prayed specifically that they would have boldness to witness in the face of persecution and that signs, wonders, and healings should be done in Jesus' name (Acts 4:29-31). God's confirming miracles make one bold for witness, for they demonstrate God's presence with his witnesses. Miracles can also convict the hearers of the gospel about the reality of the spoken Word. Thus, the Hebrew writer reminds us (2:3-4), God confirmed the apostolic witness to salvation through signs, miracles, and gifts of the Holy

Spirit. It is no different today; for the gospel to go forth in power, these various witness gifts must make it potent.

Gifts for service

Jesus often reminded his disciples that the last would be first in the kingdom, for God rewards servanthood and the love that prompts it, rather than the apparent public influence a person might have in the church. So, too, Paul reminded the Corinthians that even the insignificant gifts were vital to the life of the body. Servant gifts are common and plentiful. The people who possess them often fail to see them as a gift from God, and those who benefit from the ministries of servant gifts seldom give them due regard. This being the case, it is important that we catch the value God places upon servant gifts.

Both in Romans (12:7) and in 1 Peter (4:11), the gift of service is mentioned immediately after the gift of proclamation. Both in terms of the context (where it stands as a general contrast to preaching ministry) and in terms of the word used in the original (the word from which we derive "deacon" in English), "service" is probably a general designation for all types of more practical, physical ministries. It covers the total range of ministries to people's needs beyond the spoken word. This is a very broad area, and its possibilities are far from exhausted by some of the specific examples appearing in the biblical lists.

Those who show mercy (Romans 12:8) and those who help others (1 Corinthians 12:28) are likely the same class of people. These are those who minister to the sick and the poor, not only by medical help and material aid, but also by espousing their cause and becoming advocates for improving their lot in life. One notes the appropriateness of Paul's remark that "showing mercy" should be done "cheerfully." This is surely a fitting word for those working with the ill and the poor, where so much of one's success in this ministry depends upon the attitude shown towards the recipients of the service.

It is rather striking that the gift of "helpers" (See 1 Corinthians 12:28) immediately follows that of "healers." Apparently the first century, like the present, did not see everyone healed by miraculous means. Why else would God give some the gift of caring for the sick? We ought to see more miraculous healings than we do, but ministry to those not healed is also of crucial significance. Is it not fitting that the Spirit bestows both gifts upon God's people?

Whether or not one is gifted for direct involvement with people, a person can always contribute materially so that witness and service can go forward. Paul said we are to give with liberality (Romans 12:8). This should not be confused with gifts in large amounts, as many of the wealthy can afford to give. God's standard of liberality is determined more by what is left to the giver after the offering than by the amount given. Jesus commended the widow who gave her two copper coins rather than the wealthy who emptied money bags into the offering (Mark 12:41-44). She gave sacrificially, more than she could afford, while they merely made a contribution that would not affect their lifestyle. By biblical standards, many are liberal givers who do not think of themselves in this light, while others known for their generosity may not be nearly generous enough in their stewardship of material means.

The gifts and wholistic ministry

Not only did Christ come into the world to die for every person; he also came to minister to all the needs of the human race. The church cannot hope to take the gospel to every creature unless it is equipped to minister to the total scope of people and their needs.

If the church truly has become Christ's people, it will

share God's concern for the world and will feel the compassion of Christ for hurting people. But it will also know its limitations. Unless every believer is also made a bearer of God's Spirit, there will be large numbers of people untouched by the gospel. The whole church must be thoroughly equipped if the total Christ is to be offered to the entire world.

Have mercy on me, O God,
  according to your unfailing love;
according to your great compassion
  blot out my transgressions.
Restore to me the joy of your
  salvation
and grant me a willing spirit, to
  sustain me.

Psalm 51:1, 12

10

Failure Is Not a Terminal Illness

Psalm 51:1-17; 2 Corinthians 12:1-10

Failure has a harsh sound to it in any language. The word strikes terror in the human heart, in much the same way as the word cancer evokes our worst fears. Sometimes the word failure recalls the past. It may agitate a sense of guilt or bring to mind some painful situation which stunted growth. Sometimes it focuses upon the present and some area of our beliefs, practices, or relationships that is not being handled well. It can reach into the future, some anticipated or imagined situation that we fear will be too much for us to cope with. There is little doubt that failure—the sense that something has, is, or will go amiss—is a common human problem.

The problem has its religious dimension as well. What shall the Christian do when conscious of sin? How do we come to terms with growth that is slower than we would like? How do we deal with the feeling that our best efforts in witness and service did not seem good enough? If I must experience suffering, persecution, or the frustration of difficult and unchanging circumstances, does that mean that God is angry with me or that I am not good enough to please God? At one time or another, a Christian might associate these thoughts with failure in the spiritual life.

Strange as it may seem, the fact that temptation and failure (in various forms) is the common experience of

Christians is actually good news. It is good news because it means we are not odd, and our problems are not unique. Others have had to face similar situations in the past and are facing them in the present. We can learn from their failures, especially if we can discover how God helped them in the midst of their problems. Then we no longer feel alone and cut off from aid. How thankful we should be that the Bible records the failures of God's people as well as their successes. It is good to know that, in the midst of imperfections, we are still in the company of the saints.

Abraham

If there is one virtue for which Abraham is remembered, it is his faith (Romans 4; Hebrews 11:8-19). But he was not always strong in faith. Twice he feared he would be killed so men could have his wife Sarah. So he said she was his sister, which was a half truth. In both cases God prevented the kings in question from committing adultery with Sarah, and she and Abraham escaped harm (Genesis 12:10-20; 20:1-18). When his faith for a son wavered, he accepted Sarah's suggestion and fathered Ishmael by her slave girl Hagar (Genesis 16). Yet God proved his faithfulness to Abraham and Sarah and gave them Isaac in their old age. By then Abraham had been "strengthened in his faith" (Romans 4:20). God's faithfulness carried Abraham through his faithless moments until Abraham's faith was so strong that he became the chief example of faith in the Bible. How good to know God did not abandon Abraham or His plans for him in the times of Abraham's weaknesses.

Elijah

Among the prophets of the Bible, Elijah stands out for his courage. He did not mind confronting the king and issuing him stern prophecies of judgment. On Mt. Carmel he took on the four hundred fifty prophets of Baal in a prayer contest and proved Jehovah to be the true God. Yet soon thereafter he was running for his life, in fear of the threat of Queen Jezebel. He was a classic case of prophet "burn-out." In his depression over the state of things, with the wrong side apparently winning, he felt he alone stood for God and prayed that he might die (1 Kings 19). God dealt gently with his dispirited prophet, knowing full well his failure stemmed more from physical fatigue and emotional exhaustion than it did spiritual rebellion. Soothed by the "still small voice" of God, Elijah was able to throw off his self-pity and return to the prophetic tasks with which God had charged him.

David

How much one wishes David's record did not include the events of 2 Samuel 11 and 12. Adultery and murder are so out of character for this man "after God's heart" (1 Samuel 13:14; Acts 13:22). Yet David's repentance for his evil was as thorough as any character of the Bible. In Psalm 51 we see why he was still "a man after God's heart." David accepted the responsibility for his sin even though he recognized its roots in the corrupted nature of his heart. He did not try to bribe God's favor with religious sacrifices. With brokenness of heart, he pleaded for God's forgiveness, his cleansing, and his restoration of the joy of the Holy Spirit. He did not let rebellion become a habit as Saul did; instead, he interrupted the failure of sin as soon as God convicted his heart of wrong-doing.

Mary and Martha

Scripture makes it quite clear that Mary, Martha, and Lazarus were personal friends of Jesus. He often must have enjoyed the hospitality of their home when he visited Jerusalem. Yet both Mary and Martha suffered a low point in their faith when their brother died. It seemed to them that Jesus' presence could have prevented Lazarus' death (John 11:21, 32). The anguished loss of a loved one raised inevitable questions, and they were unable to reconcile their belief in Jesus with the fact of their brother's death. Jesus was grieved by their lack of faith, but he dealt gently with them as he always did with those who sorrowed and suffered. The net result was that they came to an enlarged understanding of the resurrection in the fact of Jesus' victory over death. I suspect that John 11 is treasured among us as much for the way Jesus ministered to these sisters, trying to cope with the pain of death, as it is for its victorious hope of the resurrection.

Peter

Peter's story of denying his association with Jesus is well-known. He overestimated the strength of his love for his Lord and underestimated the strength of temptation. Twice Jesus had tried to avert this disaster for Peter. He had warned Peter that Satan would try to sift him like wheat (Luke 22:31-32). Again, in the Garden of Gethsemane, Jesus told him to pray that he would not enter into temptation (Luke 22:40). Yet Peter and the others slept, oblivious to the hour that was fast approaching. Peter's lack of prayer and spiritual perception led to his downfall. But his repentance was immediate, sincere, and lasting. Likely with his own fall in mind, he wrote 1 Peter 5:6-11. Here he counselled humility, vigilance against one's adversary, and absolute trust in God's faithfulness to his children in the time of trial.

John Mark

John Mark's failure was that which one might expect of his youth. Perhaps he did not like the role of helper. He may have felt his gifts were not utilized and appreciated. Maybe he got tired of the routine. Possibly he was homesick. At any rate he left the missionary team to return home. Paul felt his defection disqualified him from further service. His uncle Barnabas believed he deserved another chance. John Mark made good of this second chance, so well in fact that later Paul himself was forced to concede that John Mark's service met even his high standards (2 Timothy 4:11). Frequently one's youthfulness—physical and/or spiritual—will result in imperfections of life or service. But the affirming adult who offers the second chance (and more) will find that God's veterans have grown up through repeated opportunities for growth.

Paul

Paul was one of Christ's most useful ambassadors of the New Testament age. But he knew his "down moments" as well as his times of elation. He had been granted unusual spiritual experiences in his encounter with Christ. God had worked wondrous miracles through his ministry as well. There is always the danger that persons like this can begin to think too highly of themselves, or that others may think too highly of them. In his "thorn in the flesh" experience, Paul realized both of these dangers (2 Corinthians 12:1-10). God did not answer his repeated prayers to be delivered from his difficulty, whatever it was. There was a more important lesson Paul needed to learn. In Paul's weakness, God's power could better be demonstrated, for when human ability and strength cannot be the source of victory, then God is acknowledged as the source of power and glory. Paul discovered, as many have since, that the greatest moments of growth and usefulness often come out of times of suffering, weakness, and brokenness. We discover more of the power of Christ's resurrection when first we share with him in the sufferings of his death (Philippians 3:10-11).

Lessons from failure

Experience is the best of schools, though its tuition runs a bit high. Many of the lessons we learn come at great personal cost. But one must evaluate costs in terms of results. Since the lessons we learn by failure have a way of sticking with us, perhaps the costs are well worth it. Israel, for example, seemingly could not learn how to stay away from the temptations of idolatry. So God sent them into exile in Babylon for seventy years. There they learned the lesson well. As a general rule, one can say that the Jewish people have withstood the temptation of idol worship ever since the bitter lesson of exile. Seventy years of suffering, compared to several thousand idol-free years, looks like a good investment in education.

God does not plan for us to fail. He can make use of our failures, however, to teach us some valuable lessons. God redeems situations as well as people, converting minus signs into plus factors. Note some of the things God can teach us through the things we call failure.

Realistic expectations

A common problem among Christians is that they expect too little of their life in Christ, and, consequently, live as weak Christians. Some Christians, however, have the opposite problem. They expect too much of themselves as Christians. They somehow think temptation will have no power over them. Or they believe their energy for service will never run low. Some expect their emotions to play only happy tunes, with no selections from the minor key. They believe they can find a way through every battle, coming through miraculously with no scars from the fight. The borderline between faith and fantasy is not clearly drawn for these believers.

Failure in many forms is inevitable for these people until they come to more realistic expectations of themselves and a more biblically informed basis of their faith. The Bible tells us that the godly will be subject to tempta- tion, will experience the opposition of Satan, and will undergo persecution in one form or another. At the very least, we will carry the scars of these conflicts. And, if experience shows us anything, it is that no one is always a winner. Christian victory does not mean freedom from trial, nor even the guarantee of no defeats. Victory *does* mean knowing Christ's help in the midst of testing and his grace should we fail. In the history of organized baseball, there has never been a championship team that went through the entire season without a loss. Championship teams were winners in spite of their losses. The mature Christian, also, has learned how to absorb his or her losses and emerge a winner in spite of them.

Interruption of failure

We have all known teams that played very well until they suffered their first loss. After that they went into a spiral of defeat, losing to teams they should have been able to beat and committing errors they normally would not have made. The same thing often happens to people in general and to believers in their spiritual life. Failure seems to disorient and discourage, thus paving the way for a series of additional failures. Other persons, and other teams, seem capable of absorbing a failure and, after a temporary setback, come back as strong—or often stronger—than before. The difference is their ability to interrupt failure so that it does not become a habit.

One breach of conduct does not erase entirely one's Christian character. One of Satan's favorite tactics is to tell a fallen Christian, "See what a hypocrite you are. Now that you've slipped, you might as well go and live like the sinner that you really are." He probably assailed Peter somewhat in that fashion, for Jesus had told Peter, "Satan has desired to have you that he might sift you like wheat" (See Luke 22:31). Peter, instead, was melted with repentance, for his denial of Christ was out of character with the real love he had for his Lord. David's acts of adultery and murder were out of character with his being "a man after God's own heart." Both of these Bible characters sought immediate restoration to God's favor. They knew they belonged to God and were determined that sin should not become a habit, separating them from God. The Bible is full of examples of God's forgiveness when his people confessed sin. It is when they added sin to sin that they came under God's severe judgment.

One of the best ways to interrupt failure is to confess it to another Christian. Our natural instincts when we sin are usually wrong. We tend to want to keep our failure secret, for fear that people will not think of us as highly as they previously did. We want to be alone in order to repair the damage at the least social cost. This, too, is how Satan uses failure to work further defeat in our lives. If one watches a predator attack a sheep, he will notice that it first isolates the sheep from the flock. Then the sheep is truly at the predator's mercy. The Bible counsels confession to one another (James 5:16). Sharing our defeat—even persistent failure with secret sins—frequently breaks the bond of that sin in our life. For when we sense the readiness of a brother or sister to forgive us and love us, we are enabled to believe that God's love surely outdistances theirs.

Self-discovery

As illness may force us to review our lifestyle, so failure calls us to evaluate our spiritual health. We learn to know our vulnerable spots and what we must do to protect ourselves against them. If the pressure of working with children brings us apart at the seams, we are not wise to seek an avenue of service in children's ministries. If we cannot resist sweets, we are foolish to take a job in a candy factory. The list is endless. But each of us must discover by experience our areas of strength and weakness. God will always make a "way of escape," but we must discover what it is and then use it (1 Corinthians 10:13 RSV). We will experience the same failures repeatedly in our lives unless we take to heart the things that failure clearly shows us about ourselves. We can learn to avoid specific failures.

There are times when failure points out a more general spiritual condition that needs correction. Sometimes we have been treating only symptoms of our spiritual illness and not the underlying cause. In that case God often allows failure to function like exploratory surgery. He uncovers our heart and shows us the source of the disease. We may discover an unsurrendered self at the center of our failures. It may be that we are carnally minded, controlled by desires contrary to the desires of the Spirit. When things were going at least fairly well in life, we were not concerned enough to seek God's best for us. But when we are wounded in spirit, broken-hearted over some serious failure, we become open to the deep working of God's Spirit in our innermost being. Then in the words of the Psalmist, we pass through the valley of Baca and make it a place of springs (Psalms 84:6). It is then that the pain of God's discipline results in the fruit of righteousness (Hebrews 12:11). Many a person has looked back at some painful failure in life and praised God for it. For apart from that discipline, they might never have faced the depth of spiritual need in their lives. Failure can reveal a self that needs God's drastic surgery.

God's sufficiency

Every victorious Christian has learned the secret of trusting God. These people have discovered that God does not forsake us in failure, whether that be the failure of sin, of relationships, or of service. God is strong to forgive, to reconcile, to restore. God can handle our failures better then we can. It is our inactivity which frustrates the grace of God. He wants us to throw our energies into the adventure of discipleship. It is virtually impossible to keep your balance on a bicycle when it is standing still. But if it is moving, balance is quite easily maintained, although you will probably have to turn the handlebars some to do it. Likewise, God can guide and correct us while we're moving in our Christian life, but we lose our balance when we stand still. Trust gets us in motion for God and lets him keep us on course.

Difficulty and failure serve to underline Jesus' words in John 15:4-5, "Remain in me . . . for apart from me you can do nothing." The victorious Christians are those who have learned that their true strength comes from God. Like Paul's discovery through his "thorn in the flesh," they have come to realize that God's strength is most present when their strength seems to have forsaken them. It might be the trial of physical affliction, it might be the frustration of an impossible human circumstance, or it might be the disappointment that some area of service is stymied. When our trust is in God, songs of deliverance will ultimately break forth. Faith is a Christian's victory (1 John 5:4), and God will allow all kinds of experience—even failure—to come our way to purify and refine this precious commodity (1 Peter 1:6-7).

Children of the heavenly Father

Watching parents teach an infant to walk is a fascinating experience. At first they hold both hands. Then they hold one hand. Finally they step away several paces and, with outstretched arms, invite the child to come to them. The child responds to the challenge and toddles ever widening gaps to the support and affirmation of the parent. At times the child totters on the brink of falling, only to be rescued by the quick intervention of the parent. At other times he or she falls and is consoled by mom or dad before returning to the challenge. Failure is part of the process, but no wise and loving parent would discourage walking on that account.

The Christian life often seems like learning to walk. Just as Jesus invited Peter to walk the waves of the Sea of Galilee, so God invites us to walk toward him. We may fall, but he will be there to pick us up, just as Jesus rescued Peter when he began to go down. God so wants us to learn to walk that he is willing to risk our fallings. For if he cannot get us walking, we will always be oversized babies. We cannot develop Christian maturity without the risk of trying and, sometimes, the pain of failing But in the joy of walking, going from strength to strength, we find we are "coming of age" as the sons and daughters of God.

But you are a chosen people, a royal priesthood, a holy nation, a people belonging to God, that you may declare the praises of him who called you out of darkness into his wonderful light. Once you were not a people, but now you are the people of God; once you had not received mercy, but now you have received mercy.

1 Peter 2:9-10

11

Group Life and Christian Witness

John 17:6-19; 1 Peter 2:4-10

For centuries, Protestants have ridiculed monks as the epitome of ineffectual Christianity, the apt symbol of spiritual drones. (Historians know this to be an inappropriate slander on monasticism, since they are aware of the monastic contributions to scriptural preservation, music, worship, education, medicine, agriculture, and public welfare.) Even so, in the popular Christian mind there is often a feeling that the holy life somehow must be purchased at the expense of active service in the world. Is it really true that the holy life is a retreat from the world and its needs? Are saints no more relevant than museum curios?

Those who answer "yes" to these questions—and there are such people—have some basic misunderstandings about the holy life. First, there is the common Western error of over-individualization of the gospel. This view sees the Bible as addressed solely to individuals and the holy life as strictly a private matter. The pathway of holiness is seen as a solitary pilgrimage; one makes his way alone to the celestial city. This view of the holy life is not supported by Scripture.

The second error is that the holy life can be achieved only in antiseptic environments. Either we must choose to be holy but not useful in a sinful world, or we must decide upon usefulness and sacrifice holiness. But the example of Jesus is directly contrary to this notion. He left the environment perfectly conducive to holiness (i.e. heaven) to minister in an environment antagonistic to holiness (i.e., a sin-infected world), in order that he could redeem needy sinners. Jesus was the model of a holy life in service to others.

The church and the world

If the holy life is to be Christian in outlook, it must be patterned upon the example of Jesus. His life was lived with others (his disciples) and for others (a lost world). These are the fundamental goals of the holy life. The holy life is essential to the life of the church. It must also be directed toward witness and service in the world. If it fails to produce these results, then we distort the gospel with a rampant individualism and pervert sanctification into a type of monastic retreat. And while such disengagement from the world might be an error on the side of piety, it is a serious error nontheless.

Redemptive history has always involved the group— God's people and their task. Thus we have such biblical groups as Israel, the disciples, and the church. Most of the prophetic messages of the Old Testament dealt with the nation as a whole. Likewise, Jesus' instruction was for his disciples as a group, as were also the apostolic injunctions for the church. The holy life is God's vision of his people as a whole. Thus Jesus prayed that all his disciples (including those who would believe in the centuries to come—John 17:20) might be sanctified by the truth and consecrated to God's agenda for them in the world (John 17:15-19).

Both John 17 and 1 Peter 2 combine the emphases of the corporate body and the task of witness with that of the concept of holiness. These two passages become helpful background studies to the focus of this chapter. We will look at three familiar New Testament images of the church in order to discuss some of the basic issues involved with this integration of the holy life, the life of the church, and Christ's commission for his people to carry the gospel to every creature.

The church as Christ's bride

The image of the church as the "bride of Christ" is contained in several New Testament passages. It is implied in Jesus' parables—the marriage of the king's son and the ten virgins (Matthew 22:1-14; 25:1-13). Paul gives it the most explicit treatment in his discussion of Christian marriage (Ephesians 5:21-23). It is alluded to again in the book of Revelation (21:2,9; 22:17). These passages suggest several things in regard to the purity of the church.

First, they are all cast in a future reference. The marriage is yet to be, in the age to come. The church, then, is a bride-in-preparation. Christ has given himself for her so that she might be bathed in the water of the Word and presented to him in a wedding garment free from spot or wrinkle (Ephesians 5:25-27). We sense here our Lord's concern for the purity of the church. He himself is actively involved in preparing a bride according to his own specification.

Secondly, there is an appeal to faithfulness in these passages. In order to grasp all that is meant, we must recall the rites of marriage practiced by the Jewish people. The betrothal (engagement) preceded the wedding by a definite period of time. From that point on, the bride-to-be was legally considered the wife of the man, though the wedding ceremony had not yet been held nor the marriage physically consummated. If she was unfaithful during this time of betrothal, her sin was considered to be adultery.

The relationship of Christ and the church is analogous to this marriage pattern. Already the church is Christ's own, though the actual wedding day awaits the end of the age. Meanwhile, the church is expected to be faithful to the marriage agreement. This is why James called the Christian's love of the world spiritual adultery (James 4:4). There is no end of false lovers who would tempt the church to be unfaithful to her Lord in doctrine or in practice. These associations must be steadfastly resisted in the concern to be faithful to the church's marriage covenant with Christ.

Thirdly, the church must maintain its purity in relation to that which would defile. Jude warns against those who get into the Christian fellowship and become spots and blemishes on the church's feast of love (Jude 12). He further urges carefulness for the garment that gets soiled in the process of rescuing some from the evil ways which have snared them (Jude 23). Always there is the pressure of the world and its ways upon the church, seeking to make conformists of the Christians (Romans 12:1-2).

One is reminded here of the New Testament illustration of feet washing. Though a person bathed at home before attending a feast, his feet would become dirty as he walked through the streets. Thus a host would provide for the washing of his guests' feet as people arrived for the social occasion. Likewise the church, though washed by Christ in his atoning death (symbolized by baptism), needs the continual washing of the Word, lest some spot should defile the wedding garments. The once-for-all bath of regeneration does not rule out the need for the repeated washing of that part of the body which has become stained. Periods of reformation, revival, and renewal seem to have done this for the church through the centuries.

There is a reciprocal relationship between the individual and the group in regard to the holy life, somewhat like that of a surgical team. The commitment of each team member to purity in operating room procedures either contributes to, or detracts from, the group's performance in avoiding infection in the patient. The team's standards and procedures will also affect individual team members. If the commitment to non-contamination is high, then individuals on the team will feel the group's influence on their individual attitudes and actions. If the team approach becomes careless, that will also lower the concern of many of its individual members.

All Christians are members of the bride of Christ. Just like a surgical team, group performance is important. The cleanliness of the entire church affects the attitudes and the performance of each of its members. Individuals, on the other hand, must be taught to recognize the consequences of their attitudes and actions as they affect the total performance of the church. Just as surgery is more than the work of a skilled doctor working alone, so also is the purity of the church. It takes a team commitment to purity and health.

The church as Christ's body

True body life in the church, sadly enough, is often an exception rather than the rule. The reasons are many, but one of the crucial factors is the complete dominance of individualism in our thinking. Rarely do we stop to realize how much our entire approach to life revolves around personal interests. Because we pursue so many relationships with others and belong to so many groups, we think of ourselves as group-oriented. We don't realize the truth about ourselves—the truth that we often seek relationships for personal needs and use groups for personal benefits.

Unfortunately, this same mentality affects people's relationship with the church. They seek church relationships like they shop for a bargain at the store, reading the label of all the services provided and comparing the price tag accompanying it. All too often church is merely a way to add the religious dimension to life. It is not a shared expression of Christ's life in the midst of his people.

The correct symbol of the Christian life is not that of our solar system, with individual planets revolving around the sun. Rather, the body image employed by Scripture portrays individual cells, each with life in them, but corporately dependent upon the life of the body. Cut off from the body, an organ or limb cannot survive very long. Neither can the rest of the body function as it did with this deletion from its total life system. We can never experience by ourselves "the fullness of him who fills everything in every way" (Ephesians 1:23), no matter how dramatic our spiritual experiences are. That is a body-life reality, and the holy life exists for the cultivation of this group life.

The word *homothumadon* (meaning "of one heart" or "of one mind") represents well the biblical model of body life. It is illustrated in the Old Testament by the single-minded purpose of all Israel to make David king (1 Chronicles 12:33,38) and to observe the Passover under Hezekiah after it was ignored for generations (2 Chronicles 30:12). It was the complete opposite of the pitiful expression in the book of Judges, "that each one did that which was right in his own eyes." The prophets Jeremiah (32:39) and Ezekiel (11:19) prophesied of a time that God would give his people "oneness of heart" in serving the Lord.

It is absolutely astonishing to notice how frequently this expression is used in the book of Acts to describe the early Christians. They prayed with one heart (Acts 1:14; 4:24), attended the temple worship together in the same frame of mind (Acts 2:46), held a common attitude toward property and material things (Acts 4:32), and made council decisions in a united voice (Acts 15:25). Thus one of the effects of Pentecost was a binding together of the early believers so that they thought and acted as a united group.

They could be described as a group "with one mind" or "one heart." Whatever our claims to spiritual experiences and growth, if we are not drawn into a vital union with other believers, we are not realizing the unity of the body that accompanies the biblical picture of the holy life.

Unity does not mean sameness, for the body has many parts with different functions. Yet these various organs are not at cross-purposes with each other. A single purpose pervades the body, each part doing its function for the health of the whole body. Likewise the goal of the holy life in the church is to produce a single-minded devotion to the cause of Christ. In order to accomplish this, members must be encouraged to sacrifice individual agendas for the greater good of the group and the ministry it must fulfill. The work of the kingdom is such that it can only be accomplished if everyone shares the vision of God's will for the church and devotes himself or herself to it with single-minded purpose.

There have been times in the history of the church when a profound sense of unity made the church potent in its witness. The history of the Moravian Church is interesting in this regard. Torn by disputes and doctrinal factions, the people were brought to a compact of external peace by the efforts of Count Zinzendorf. But they sensed a need for an inner harmony to bind them together. They began to pray for a spirit of unity. While in a communion service at the village church of Berthelsdorf on August 17, 1727, their prayer was answered. The Spirit of God was poured out upon them, and they found themselves bound together by a sense of love and fellowship like they had never experienced before. They subsequently became a leading missionary movement of the eighteenth century. One of the things that impressed people who came into contact with the Moravians was the sense of love and unity which characterized their fellowship. Is not this a true, biblical Pentecost?

Keith Miller has referred to local churches as outposts of the kingdom. The realities of the eternal world are not easily grasped. How shall unbelievers be convicted of the very existence of these realities unless the church is a living proof of them? When brothers and sisters truly love each other, bear one another's burdens, worship together, and meet the physical and material needs among them, then a sense of Christ's body emerges. Jesus prayed (John 17) that such would be the case, so that his own would be preserved in the world and that the unsaved would come to believe that Jesus was the Christ. And this sense of the body is what emerged in the early church. The book of Acts is not only a description of how rapidly the church grew in numbers; it is also the story of a fantastic fellowship that developed in the church. There evangelism and fellowship complemented each other.

The church as Christ's building

Every building is constructed with some purpose in mind. It is built to be a residence, a business, a school, a place of storage, a recreational facility, or an artistic expression. When 1 Peter 2:4-10 talks of the church as a building, obviously comparing it to the Jewish temple in Jerusalem, it is emphasizing the functional goal of the church. The church has a task to accomplish; it was designed and constructed to declare the good news of Jesus to people everywhere.

Peter's description of the church as Christ's building has several suggestions to make to us along this line. First, he says emphatically that people are the church. Christ is the chosen, precious cornerstone. His people are living stones joined to and aligned by him, thus composing God's true temple in the world. Christ's church is not a physical structure, nor merely an organizational entity. It is a spiritual structure—people made alive by the Spirit. It needs organization, but it is not confined to any historic denomination. The beautiful thing about this is that God's church is present wherever his people are. This church becomes visible wherever his people touch those who need to become God's people.

Secondly, the people are a company of priests. Christianity no more has a special group of people indispensable for one's salvation than it has one temple where God can supposedly be met. Instead, every Christian has been made a priest of God, a witness to the gospel of Jesus Christ. The implications of this are tremendous. On one hand, it means the code of holiness imposed only upon priests in the Old Testament is now required of all God's people. On the other hand, it means that there are priests in every location and occupation. A priestly caste would be out of place in many segments of society. But when the miner, store clerk, judge, banker, nurse, or farmer next to you is a priest of God, then God comes near to you in your language, clothes, and life experiences. The Christian company of priests is intended to make Jesus the Immanuel for every human being.

Thirdly, the priests are proclaimers of the gospel. Their job is to "declare the praises of him who called you out of darkness into his wonderful light" (1 Peter 2:9). One does not need to be highly trained in theology, nor schooled in priestly ritual, to perform this spiritual service. We merely tell our story: how God took the darkness, chaos, and emptiness of life away and made us his own child. The most potent advertising media for Christianity is not the printed page; neither is it radio, television, nor film. It is the countless stories of men and women who tell about the difference Jesus makes in their life. These flesh and blood ads proclaim the good news of salvation.

A matter of perspective

Infants seem to start life with a world view limited to their own personal needs. In the process of socialization, children become increasingly aware of their family and the world of people beyond. They still have personal needs, but they must find their fulfillment in the recognition of the needs that others have and their responsibility to be a "giver" as well as a "receiver" in life. The word "others" takes on an increasingly important dimension in their vocabulary.

Ask a given individual at different stages in his Christian life why he is a Christian, and you probably will not get the same answer. In the first stage of commitment he might well answer, "Because Christ alone meets my need for salvation." While that foundational reason never goes away, many other reasons will be laid on top of that confession, like so many blocks upon a building's foundation. As one follows the layers of reasons that are built up, he will discover that group language and service language become more prominent in one's awareness of why he is a Christian.

The purpose of the holy life is to help us make the transition from the perspective of a "babe in Christ" to that of a mature disciple. The pace of this change and the experiences necessary to effect it will vary with the individual in question. God's intention for all his people, however, is abundantly clear. He wants to transform the "person focus" of our life from the singular "I" to the plural forms "we" and "they." The degree to which these various points of focus control our reason for living will be about as accurate a measure of our maturity as can be found.

I pray also that the eyes of your heart may be enlightened in order that you may know the hope to which he has called you, the riches of his glorious inheritance in the saints, and his incomparably great power for us who believe.

Ephesians 1:18-19

12

The Tug of the Future

Matthew 25:31-46; Ephesians 1:15-23

There are people who cannot resist reading the last chapter of a book to see how it concludes before reading the rest of the story. They do not have the patience to let a plot develop, nor can they stand the suspense that surrounds their hero—they must know in advance if things will have a happy ending. In that way they can discount every complexity, shrug off every foil, and see through each sad part in the knowledge that "happy ever after" already is the destined end of the story.

While this can be criticized as a bad way of treating literature, there is a qualified sense in which it is an appropriate approach to spiritual things. Spiritual issues are the matters of the greatest importance—in these matters one needs to know how a particular course of action will pan out. God's future is the only certain future. We need to place the uncertainties of our story within the context of his story.

God's blueprint

Jesus came preaching the kingdom of God. He got people to make life choices on the basis of eternal realities. The first petitions of the prayer he gave his disciples were "They kingdom come, Thy will be done." Thus the Christian life begins with the future ("Thy kingdom come"), then steps back from that to the present ("Thy will be done"). The resurrection of Jesus has given the future more leverage on our life than the past we have experienced. So much of popular psychology is mired in people's past and how that has shaped and scarred them. Jesus offers pardon from our past and releases us for the future he has prepared for us. The vision of the people he will make us, rather than the memory of what we were, is the mental image that he wants to dominate our life.

God's future for us is like an architect's blueprint. The ordinary laborer might not envision the total building. He understands his own trade, be it masonry, carpentry, plumbing, electrical, or whatever; but he does not comprehend fully the interrelation of the parts nor the necessary sequence of the processes. However, he can follow the blueprint and carry out his responsibility. As the several craftsmen do likewise, the building will be completed according to the design envisioned by the original architect. None of us grasps the complete future as God does, but we can learn to read the part of the blueprint that relates to us. The purpose of the holy life is to build according to God's blueprint in our own life and in the life of the church.

Paul's prayer for enlightenment

One can sense the power of the future in Paul's prayer for the church in the first chapter of the letter to the Ephesians. He prayed that believers would be enlightened to see three things: (1) the hope to which God has called them, (2) the inheritance of Christ in his people; and (3) the great resurrection power which is already at work in the believer's life. The first two of these relate directly to the future as a blueprint for the present. The third item relates to the present work of the Holy Spirit in the church, moving God's people forward to the ultimate goal of the fulfilled kingdom.

The hope of our calling

The Apostle Paul's personal example illustrates that which he prayed would become true for all Christians. Before he met Christ on the road to Damascus (Acts 9), his life was shaped by a past which made him hostile to the entire Christian enterprise. Then he saw Christ. Paul's great purpose from that point on was to pursue the knowledge of Christ and the ultimate prize of heaven. Like a magnet attracts iron objects to itself, so this hopeful vision pulled Paul along toward its fulfillment. Paul had read life's final chapter, in which God revealed to him the glorious outcome of the people of God. Paul wanted his fellow Christians to experience a similar enlightenment so that they, too, might enjoy the blessings of such an outlook.

It is the hope of the Christian's calling which often sustains the present. Some things in life are endured only because we have hope that they shall end, that God will again turn our sorrow into song. Thus, the Psalmist was sustained by his confidence that he would "see the goodness of the Lord in the land of the living." It enabled him to "be strong and take heart and wait for the Lord" (Psalm 27:13, 14).

While the Christian faith is much more than "pie in the sky bye and bye," the ability to believe in God's final redemption is often the "iron in the blood" that the Christian needs to endure what is difficult in the present. Paul put it well in Romans 8:18-25. We often groan under the burden of life in a fallen world, hoping—as those who have experienced the "first fruits" of the gospel—for the redemption of our bodies. It is by this hope that we are saved again and again from overwhelming burdens. This is particularly true when we, like Job, suffer the inexplicable.

Paul's testimony in this regard is found in 2 Corinthians 4. He writes of his afflictions, perplexities, persecutions, and loneliness, but says he is not crushed, driven to despair, forsaken, nor destroyed. The reason is given in verses 16-18:

> Therefore we do not lose heart. Though outwardly we are wasting away, yet inwardly we are being renewed day by day. For our light and momentary troubles are achieving for us an eternal glory that far outweighs them all. So we fix our eyes not on what is seen, but on what is unseen. For what is seen is temporary, but what is unseen is eternal.

Paul saw through the things that were happening to him at the time and realized that God was using them for his future good. Faith guaranteed an ending which made it possible for him to undergo the present.

The hope of our calling gives meaning and purpose to our present development in holy living. If, in the end, the godly character (i.e., the fruit of the Spirit) would prove to be of no merit, who would concern himself with it? But if the character God brings to fruition in us is found to be the stuff fit for heaven, then all our diligence in godly living is abundantly repaid. A medical student endures the rigor of his preparation in the hope of being a doctor; there is a direct relationship between the preparation and the product. So, too, for the Christian. One continues to grow in grace for the sake of being among those presented to the Father with great joy as being "holy and blameless" in Christ's love. The things of the Spirit—faith, hope, and love—endure in the eternal order (1 Corinthians 13:13). The hope of our calling affirms that these are the permanent things, the things which outlast the present age.

God's future also stimulates our present as we press forward to that which awaits us. When a date is determined for a wedding, the birth of a child, or the beginning of a new job, one does not sit by in idleness, letting the future come at its leisure. No, the anticipation of what will be brings about all kinds of preparation. We do not want to be caught unprepared and unaware. To the best of our ability we make every reasonable preparation for that which is about to happen. So, too, the holy life is spiritual development tugged along by the future. As children race toward completion of pencil sketches, as their lines connecting the numbered dots reveal the identity of the figure, so we press forward most earnestly when our eye has grasped God's future for us.

Picture a person, crippled by an injury, who has experienced partial restoration through physical therapy. It would be hard for us to imagine that person turning down additional therapy which could bring complete wholeness. Similarly, can the Christian be satisfied with the first fruits of the Spirit—the foretaste of eternal inheritance (Ephesians 1:13-14)—and not the final harvest, when all things will be complete in Christ? Great as the benefits of God's grace are in this life, they are but tokens of greater things to come. The lure of the eternal—the perfect and the complete—inhabits the human spirit. Christianity vitalizes this desire and makes it a servant of the Christian's faith.

We see many examples of people who live rich, meaningful lives because they have stored up the treasures of the past and live off the interest it affords. By faith the Christian does also. All the saving acts of God throughout biblical history, as well as the experiences of God's grace in one's own past, provide the resources from which one lives day to day. But Christianity is unique in that it can make the treasury of the future available to the present as

well. Christ is Lord of time; he inhabits the future as well
as the present. In him the future is already breaking into
our present, and we live off its interest without diminish-
ing one bit the reality of its principal. The Christian faith,
therefore, is without apology for its future orientation, for
it enriches the present without distracting us from it.

Christ's inheritance in the saints

The second thing Paul prayed for the Ephesians was
that they would be enlightened to understand the inheritance of Christ in his people. Christ, though rich, became
poor for our sake in order that we could become rich (2
Corinthians 8:9). He laid aside the benefits of his equality
with the Father in order to become the humble, human
servant that went to the death of a shameful cross (Philippians 2:5-8). In this way he was reduced to poverty that we
might inherit the wealth of eternal salvation.

In doing this, Christ linked his inheritance to that of
the redeemed. He is the seed which has fallen upon human
hearts, perchance to produce forty-, sixty-, or a hundred-
fold (Matthew 13:1-9, 18-23). He distributed his wealth to
his servants, while he returned to heaven to await all his
enemies being put under his feet (Matthew 25:14-30).
Some of his servants will not cause his investment to
grow. But others will increase it five-fold or ten-fold.
Whenever Christ's disciples worship the "name above
every name," witness to the name that brings salvation, or
work for him to whom the kingdom belongs, they are
providing Christ an abundant inheritance in his saints
(Philippians 2:9-11). It is a sobering thought to realize that
the neglect of Christian duty diminishes the inheritance
which is due to Christ. Well ought Christian eyes be
enlightened to realize how they might devote themselves
to the things that exalt the glory of Christ's name.

Here is where the passage regarding the sheep and

the goats (Matthew 25:31-46) has particular bearing. When Jesus became man, subject to the limitations and pain of human existence, he demonstrated God's concern for the lost of mankind. He experienced hunger, thirst, and pain. He was thrust into prison and condemned to an unjust death. At his crucifixion he was deprived of the only clothes he could justly call his own. All this is a matter of historical record. But it is more. In Christ, God has identified himself with those who suffer similar conditions in their sojourn in life.

Thus, whatever we do to relieve human distress is really done to Christ. When we feed the hungry, clothe the naked, visit the imprisoned, give hospitality to the strangers and the destitute, and care for the sick, we are doing these things to Christ. If we catch what the Lord is saying here, we cannot dismiss these obligations as mere "social gospel" stuff. This is basic discipleship! If we love our Lord, we will do these things as a love service to him. And if we ignore such duties, the message is plain: we do not love our Lord. The Apostle John minced no words: "If anyone has material possessions and sees his brother in need but has no pity on him, how can the love of God be in him?" (1 John 3:17). "For anyone who does not love his brother, whom he has seen, cannot love God, whom he has not seen" (1 John 4:20b). The punishment upon the goats (Matthew 25), then, is just. Their lack of compassionate ministry reflects the fact that they know nothing of God's love and, therefore, do not really belong to him.

Some of us have had the experience of being invited to a social function without the clear understanding that gifts were expected. Our embarrassment was even worse if the gathering was some sort of Christmas celebration in which there were gifts intended for us, even though we had none to give in return. It is not hard to imagine our chagrin at the heavenly feast at the end of the age should we come with nothing to offer to Christ, while all the benefits of the eternal world are prepared for us. At the moment when we will realize most fully how greatly Christ enriched us through his grace, we will feel most keenly the lack of our service for the cause of his kingdom in doing the things that would have enriched his inheritance in the saints.

Given the depth of human need, the gospel must begin with the good news of salvation—the hope of our calling. But it does not—and it dare not—stop there, or the great gift of salvation would be consumed entirely upon our own selfish desires. Somehow Christians must realize that they are "bought at a price" (1 Corinthians 6:19-20) and consequently owe everything to the one who redeemed them. The dream of our future must be harmonized fully with God's future and his plan to sum up everything in Jesus Christ. One of the great tests of Christian maturity is the degree to which our aspirations— our reasons for living—are identical with the will of God as realized in the kingdom of Christ.

If our eyes are truly opened to see the cause of Christ's kingdom, then we will want to "make the most of every opportunity"—literally we will "buy up" every chance to do good (Ephesians 5:16). Our opportunity might be to offer the "cup of water in Christ's name" to one who is thirsty (Matthew 10:42) or to share the good news about Jesus so that someone comes to know that inward "spring of water welling up to eternal life" (John 4:14). It might be cooperating with an organized network of international Christian aid like Mennonite Central Committee or World Vision International. Or it could be an individual in a local church who keeps up the house repairs for a widow near at hand. Whether we minister to physical or spiritual needs, as individuals or as groups, we are doing it for Christ and the kingdom he is establishing.

It is not that the works of our hands establish the kingdom by human means alone. It is always Christ who builds the kingdom, but he invites us to have a share in his work. He works through us to minister to people in need. Neither will we establish by our efforts some ideal social order that replaces the need for heaven. Quite the opposite—it is precisely the fact that we feel the pull of God's future upon us, and upon our world, which gets us involved in doing the things which will endure when everything else is gone. The urgency of the kingdom is that Christ is coming soon. We must have our understanding enlightened, therefore, to know what use of our time and resources can best accomplish the things he most wants us to do. For soon we shall see the King of this kingdom, and he will say: "I tell you the truth, whatever you did for one of the least of these brothers of mine, you did for me" (Matthew 25:40).

God's great power in us

Paul's final petition in this prayer helps us get things in proper perspective. Jesus' death conquered the powers of this age—the formidable forces that oppose the kingdom. His resurrection opened the doors of paradise so that the power of the eternal order could be released in our age. Already the Spirit of eternity is at work in the world, subjecting all things on behalf of the good of the church. We are far from being helpless in the face of what needs to be done. The Holy Spirit is the power of God at work in the church.

One of the great problems in relation to the holy life is that Christians often are tempted to diminish the impact of the hope of their calling by postponing its fulfillment to some indefinite future. Struck by the realities of their present condition and feeling the resistance to making the changes which discipleship demands, it is easy to exchange faith in the present age for hope in the age to come. If we believe that the mature Christian life is possible only in heaven, then we can shrug off the urgent call to attain it in this present life.

But the Bible does not use the hope of heaven as an escape clause from the implications of discipleship. Jesus told many parables about the kingdom which is coming, but his punch line was always, "be ye therefore ready." His true disciples would be those who did their Lord's bidding while they awaited his return (Matthew 24:45-51). The apostles struck a similar chord. In his second letter Peter has much to say about the Lord's coming and the end of the age, but his appeal is that Christians would be careful to live godly lives now in preparation for that day (2 Peter 3:10-14). John's first epistle moves quickly from the promise that "we shall be like him" when we "see him as he is" to the application that those possessed of that hope should purify themselves now to be pure as Jesus is pure (1 John 3:1-3). In every case the anticipated future is seen as that which spurs on development of the holy life in the present.

The case is similar in regard to the kingdom service which fulfills Christ's inheritance in the saints. One can easily become discouraged about the deplorable state of the world. Evil appears to have an iron grip upon people everywhere and has infested every human structure. How can the massive problems of hunger, sickness, joblessness, oppression, and war be solved? They touch so many people in such extensive ways that we may feel our efforts, however noteworthy, would be but a mere drop in the bucket. Evangelism seldom keeps pace with the world's population growth, and social programs often seem to be too little aid to too few of the world's needy. How can we overcome the feeling that the attempt to solve human need is like throwing feathers into the wind?

The key to realizing the power of God presently at

work in the church is to notice the relationship Scripture establishes between Christ and his people. Usually we note Paul's description of this power in terms of Christ's resurrection from the dead and his ascension to the right hand of God, the seat of authority over all things (Ephesians 1:19-23). But to catch the full significance of the message, we must follow Paul's discussion into the opening verse of Ephesians 2. Here we realize that we, too, were raised with Christ and seated with him in the heavenly realms (Ephesians 2:6). Our lot is so closely joined to his that Christ's victories become ours as well. Already, as his people, we participate in his triumph over evil.

Perhaps the story of Joseph (Genesis 37-50) can help us catch the point. When he was rescued from Pharaoh's prison by God's power and raised to the seat of authority next to Pharaoh, it happened not only for him, but also for his people. As he later explained to his brothers, God had allowed this for the salvation of Israel, because he was thereby placed in a position of power where he could provide for Israel the things necessary for life. Thus his exaltation meant theirs as well. They, like he, had access to all the resources of the monarch of Egypt.

The lot of the Christians is exactly like this. Second Peter 1:3 puts it well: "His divine power has given us everything we need for life and godliness through our knowledge of him who called us by his own glory and goodness." Everything necessary for the development of our spiritual life and for the work of the kingdom in this age is ours in Christ. In him we have access to all the resources of God. We will still encounter the opposition of the evil powers of this world system (Ephesians 6:12), but we do so with the full armor provided for us (Ephesians 6:10-20). God's resources are more than adequate for our needs.

For the church, the kingdom of God is already present; what remains for the future is to subject all other kingdoms to this rule of God. We feel this tug of heaven upon our lives because the future has already invaded our present and has firmly grasped us. The final chapter of history is already written: God is going to unite everything in Jesus Christ (Ephesians 1:10). For those of us already united with Christ, the knowledge of how the story ends is just what we need to see us through the remaining chapters of world history. We are not among the power-less and dispossessed of the earth. We are citizens of the kingdom, yes, even members of the King's own household (see Ephesians 2:19). No wonder Paul urgently prayed that Christians would have their eyes open to perceive God's "incomparably great power for us who believe" (Ephesians 1:19). Salvation in Christ makes all the re-sources of God's power available to the church.

Promoted to glory

In a cemetery in London's East End, one will find the graves of William and Catherine Booth, founders of the Salvation Army which did so much to redeem this slum community of the city. Their gravestones record the usual information of their birthdates. They differ, however, in recording the date of their deaths. Instead of the ordinary "died on _____," their headstones read "promoted to glory on _____." In the style of the Salvationists, one's death was viewed as the last promotion to the highest rank possible in the army of the Lord.

Every analogy must end somewhere. The process of human life has served us well as an extended analogy throughout this study of the holy life. It began with the comparison of conversion to the miracle of human birth. We have viewed various stages and developments of life, both physical and spiritual, in pursuit of maturity. But now we come to a halt. Natural life comes to an end in death; spiritual life does not. Death for the Christian is real, but transitional. It finds not the cessation of life, but the fulfillment of it in the eternal kingdom. The holy life has no end; it simply undergoes a transition from this life to eternal life. The Christian life concludes not with a death certificate but with a promotion to glory. Hallelujah!